WATCH THIS
LISTEN UP
CLICK HERE

WATCH THIS
LISTEN UP
CLICK HERE

INSIDE THE 300 BILLION DOLLAR BUSINESS
BEHIND THE MEDIA YOU CONSTANTLY CONSUME

DAVID VERKLIN
BERNICE KANNER

John Wiley & Sons, Inc.

Published by John Wiley & Sons, Inc., Hoboken, New Jersey.
Published simultaneously in Canada.

Wiley Bicentennial Logo: Richard J. Pacifico

For general information on our other products and services or for technical support, please contact our Customer Care Department within the United States at (800) 762-2974, outside the United States at (317) 572-3993 or fax (317) 572-4002.

Designations used by companies to distinguish their products are often claimed by trademarks. In all instances where the author or publisher is aware of a claim, the product names appear in Initial Capital letters. Readers, however, should contact the appropriate companies for more complete information regarding trademarks and registration.

Wiley also publishes its books in a variety of electronic formats. Some content that appears in print may not be available in electronic books. For more information about Wiley products, visit our web site at www.wiley.com.

Library of Congress Cataloging-in-Publication Data:

Verklin, David.
    Watch this, listen up, click here : inside the 300 billion dollar business behind the media you constantly consume / David Verklin, Bernice Kanner.
        p.   cm.
    ISBN 978-0-470-05643-1 (cloth)
        1. Advertising—United States.   2. Mass media—United States.   I. Kanner, Bernice.   II. Title.
    HF5813.U6V47   2007
    659.10973—dc22

                                                                                2007002544

Printed in the United States of America.

10   9   8   7   6   5   4   3   2   1

To my wife Veronica, an inspiration and life partner; to my children Ryan, Timothy, and Catherine, in the hope that they pursue their passions; and to my mother and father, Bob and Vivienne Verklin—my greatest fortune was to be their son.

—David Verklin

Bernice Kanner was an exceptional friend, mother, wife, reader, and sportswoman, but her true passion was writing. This, her last book, is a memorial to her great enthusiasm for everything she undertook. She is still alive within its pages.

—Lisy Cuming, daughter of Bernice Kanner

CONTENTS

PREFACE

Thanks for glancing.

That's really all I need from you. Guys like me will pay you for your glance. What I'm really after, however, is something more—something we call *engagement*. I'll reward you bigtime for that, as I'll explain in the pages ahead.

I am sitting on JAL flight #1553 on my way home from Shanghai. I've spent the last week here meeting colleagues, clients, and prospective clients and reviewing the operations and performance of the 40 companies that my employer, Aegis Group plc, owns and operates in the Asia Pacific region. Aegis isn't top of mind, nor is Carat of which I'm CEO, yet we're the fourth largest buyer of advertising time and space in the world. Have you seen an ad for Pfizer, Radioshack, Hyundai, Kia, Pringles, Iams, Bounty, or Motorola? Then we've met. I'm the guy who put them in your line of sight.

I am tired from this 20-hour trip with a connection via Tokyo, but energized by the incredible changes happening around the globe right before our eyes in the world of commercial persuasion. Take a guess: Which country currently has the most mobile phones in use? Everyone you know has a cell phone, so you'd probably think the United States. Which country has the largest percentage of its population hooked up with high-speed Internet connections? Again, you might think the United States, or some country in Europe, like Germany. You'd be wrong on both counts. China has more cell phones in use today than the population of the United States. Over 300 million Chinese citizens have a wireless communications device at this writing and that number is growing at an astronomical rate. (According to the Census Bureau the U.S. population only hit the 300 million mark on October 17, 2006.) As for high-speed Internet connections or broadband, the leader in the club-house is South Korea: Over 80 percent of its citizens have access to the Internet with full-motion video and rapid connectivity.

In his marvelous book, *The World Is Flat*, Tom Friedman brilliantly explains that we now live in a world where competition knows no borders. The authors of *Freakonomics* show how the old supply-and-demand model of economics can no longer explain the way business now behaves and transacts. Bernice and I wrote this book to explain the way the media and communications business works and the changes that are taking place in it to show you how the days of passively waiting, reading, watching, and receiving information are gone. In the world of commercial persuasion, most of the media around you will collapse and die in short order. You are now in control of what, when, how, and where you consume information and entertainment. Here's a user's manual for understanding the media around you. Forget the blinking lights of your unset VCR; we are moving into a world where the communications possibilities are disruptive, disconcerting, and oh, so exciting.

And so accessible and part of your life—it's all right there in front of your very eyes every day. Have you ever wondered why the TV show you love got canceled and what you can't stand stays on? Why are there so many commercials on the radio, and why did Howard Stern leave terrestrial for satellite? And what is satellite radio, and why would anyone pay for radio when you can get it free whenever you want?

The money to oil the American media machine comes from two basic sources: One of them is you (who pays your cable TV bill, buys your movie ticket, and stops at the newsstand for a magazine or newspaper?). But the real financial engine powering what you watch, read, and listen to comes from guys like me and the clients I represent in the business of planning and buying advertising campaigns.

From now on, please consider that every time that you see an ad, someone like me working for a company like mine has made a conscious effort, using incredibly sophisticated research, computer software, and analytics, to put it there and to reach out and touch someone just like you. As the buyers of time and space, in some sense we control what TV programs you get to watch, what magazines continue to get published, and how Google and Yahoo! stay in (very healthy) business. It's a simple Faustian bargain that you've made, but one with enormous implications. The TV program coming into your living room isn't free.

David Verklin
April 2007

I first approached David Verklin with the idea to write a book about the nine men and one woman who buy the advertising that essentially controls what we see and hear. I'd known him for more than 20 years as he made his way up the media-buying ladder to the apex as one of the principal gatekeepers of billions of advertisers' dollars. Within 90 minutes of that meeting, as the day outside his 32nd-floor office at Park and 34th ebbed into evening, we'd decided to dismiss the other nine and go it alone, revealing the behind-the-scenes tribulations of media minders as their landscape morphs before their eyes into something they wouldn't have recognized a mere five years ago.

I had written about marketing for more than two decades, first at *Advertising Age*, then for 13 years in the "On Madison Avenue" column at *New York* magazine, and after that at Bloomberg, but rarely had I delved into media. Even my marketing books, *The 100 Best TV Commercials and Why They Worked*, *The Super Bowl of Advertising: How the Commercials Won the Game*, and *Pocketbook Power: Marketing to the World's Most Coveted Consumers*, skirted what I'd considered an arcane backwater of gross rating points and HUT levels. Dissecting how a commercial got us to buy—that was sexy. Delving into algorithms was math.

Then, on cat's paws, media stealthily stole the show. What *how* was during the ad industry's Creative Revolution of the 1970s, *where* became in the twenty-first century. Media became the hub of the trillion-dollar marketing and advertising world and David Verklin was the hub within that hub.

I was hardly the only one recognizing that. In the October 10, 2005, issue of *Advertising Age*, editor Scott Donaton praised his guts and willingness to take a public stand, mused about his "devilish smile, radio voice and urgent delivery," and wondered whether there was "really . . . a single other human being who has been as much of a leader, visionary, a force for change and a voice of optimism in the marketing and media industries over the last 15 years" as David Richard Verklin.

I don't think there has been, but I do think I'm awfully lucky to join him in his crusade.

Bernice Kanner
September 2006

ACKNOWLEDGMENTS

Writing a book is never a solitary endeavor. Writing one about a world in flux requires the help of many experts. Luckily for us, Carat has them in droves.

For their invaluable information and guidance we want to heartily thank: Andy Donchin, Mitch Oscar, Audrea Fulton, Todd Hansen, Scott Sorokin, John Cate, Jason Acker, Dennis McGuire, Pearl Kim, Molina Beck, Mike Yudin, Randy Stone, Mike Reisman, Dale Tesmond, Gene Keenan, Michael Nicholas, Susan Rowe, Ginger Taylor-White, Johann Wachs, Jeremy Cornfeldt, Renny Gleeson, Bill Mungovan, Ralph Folz, Sarah Potemkin, Roy Currlin, and Geoff Thatcher.

For their immensely valuable help in fact-checking we wish to thank Jennifer Clark, Lisa D'Innocenzo, Emmy Xida, and Lisbeth Sinclair.

For the overall support of the project, our gratitude to Virginia Hanchar, Simon Zinger, Elizabeth Corradino, Adrienne Scordato, Paul Williamson, Tracy Pearce, Nicole Torres, and Jan-Marie Bannon.

For technical help, our thanks to Andrew Cuming.

For trafficking, midwifery, and overall shepherding this out the door, enormous gratitude to Nicole Marsh.

And for help picking up and mending broken pieces, thanks go to Lisy Cuming.

SPECIAL
ACKNOWLEDGMENT

Bernice Kanner conceived the idea for this book and put her heart and soul into making it happen. She passed away a few weeks after we delivered the completed manuscript to the publisher. She was a smart, funny, and passionate observer of media, advertising, and culture, and this book will be part of her legacy.

—David Verklin

PART ONE

THE LAY OF MEDIALAND

1

YOU WATCHED 33 HOURS OF TV LAST WEEK, DIDN'T YOU?

I f *you* didn't, someone else did and then some, because 33 hours a week is the national average. Many people spend more time watching than they do working—yet TV is hardly our only media obsession. Almost two-thirds of our waking life—around $10\frac{1}{2}$ hours a day—we're engaged with media. The average adult spends 2 hours and 54 minutes each day listening to radio, an earful that jumps to 5 hours on weekends. Another 45 minutes is devoted to leafing through magazines, and 25 minutes flipping through newspapers. Factor in the time we spend in cyberspace (14 hours a week depending on gender) and video games (another hour a week), and we're talking real commitment here. By 2008, media should consume more than 11 hours of our day, and that's not counting the time we spend multitasking.

And we are communicating back: The media wall that kept marketers and those marketed to apart for generations has been torn down with a lot less fanfare than the Berlin Wall. A kind of digital democracy is bringing us together to choose which ads we see and where we see them. Marketers will know what we like because we'll tell them. Today, "we have to think of everything as a collaborative medium," Procter & Gamble (P&G) CEO A. G. Lafley says. "The customer is now [also] the marketer."

Where we are spending our time is growing ever more diverse as more media platforms serve up a smorgasbord of offerings. (Special events like the Super Bowl still keep *everyone* gathered around the electronic hearth.)

Most of it, like broadcast TV and Internet searches, *seems* free, but marketers actually foot the bill. Their advertising dollars bring us the *Oscars* and *C.S.I.* They subsidize Civil War buffs' online digging, our access to movie reviews, and driving directions, and pay for news coverage of political elections, deadly tsunamis, and daily train delays, albeit indirectly. In 2005, their "subsidy" worldwide amounted to $148.2 billion. Half of that—$74 billion—was spent in the United States.

This means that we're exposed to an estimated 3,000 ads a day. That's counting highway billboards, posters in trains, buses, and bathroom stalls, commercials in movie theaters, holograms on buildings and taxis, "talking" grocery shelves, and stickers on food (CBS has stamped eggs with ads for its shows). But that doesn't take into account all the bumper stickers, t-shirt slogans, and ads on people's anatomy that we see (yes, Dunkin' Donuts paid college kids to panel their foreheads with messages about great coffee). And that 3,000-ad tally doesn't count the now almost ubiquitous product placements embedded in films, TV shows, and games.

No wonder some are calling this the Age of Interruption. Commercial avoidance has become a high art. Seven out of 10 people wish they could *will* the ads away. But it's not the advertising they hate as much as the uninvited disruption.

Not so long ago, figuring out where to interrupt (that is, place ads) wasn't all that hard. In 1965, Procter & Gamble launched Scope by buying four weeks of ads on the big three TV networks—ABC, CBS, and NBC. P&G and Scope reached more than 90 percent of television households, not once, but 10 times over. Back then, when Madison Avenue was the physical heartland of the industry and not an abstract embodiment of it, marketing's big decision was whether to buy 30-second TV commercials, full or half-pages in magazines, highway billboards, or minutes on morning or afternoon radio drive time. Advertisers chose the time and place to present their story to, if not a captive audience, at least a somewhat passive one.

The three networks that once reached 90 percent of households simultaneously now reach less than a third of that. The Web-based world of video cell phones, blogs, iPods, MP3s, BlackBerries, Treos, and Palm Pilots has put the kibosh on passive audiences receiving advertising for products they don't need. In this new era of search and choice, brand democratization, and citizen marketing, you control what you see and hear. Why should you sit through a dog food commercial if Polly wants a cracker?

That has had serious implications for marketers. Consider how P&G, which invented the soap opera as a vessel to carry news about Scope, now markets Folgers coffee with a witty microsite (toleratemornings.com) and a wacky viral music video clip (with lyrics like "You can sleep when you are dead") distributed via YouTube.com.

Tectonic changes are roiling the media beyond the advent of new platforms to serve up content and ads. As marketers scramble to stay ahead (or at least abreast) of the technological innovations that are changing how people receive messages, those who plan and buy media have become the industry's rock stars and oracles. The ads themselves now play second fiddle to where they're presented.

The advertising universe has transformed itself, bifurcating into companies that create the ads themselves and media services companies that buy the time and space. Massive consolidation has left 10 giants, many unknown just five years ago, in control of the global business of buying advertising time and space. Three out of every four network TV commercials sold in the upfront (the time when ad commitments are made for the following year) this year in America were bought by six companies—that's over $9 billion of time. Almost 80 percent of Time Inc.'s revenue now comes from seven big media services companies. None—not Starcom, Mindshare, OMD, Universal-McCann, or Carat—existed before 1998 in the United States. Where did they come from?

In 1981, Gilbert Gross, a Frenchman who's a world-class poker champion and looks like a cross between Walter Matthau and Jean Paul Belmondo, owned a small Parisian ad agency. Gross hit on a simple idea: Buy media in volume, get volume pricing, and resell it—the first media brokerage. He was so successful that if an advertiser wanted to get on the airwaves in France, it had to go to Gross. His company was the precursor of Carat, an acronym for Centrale (companies) d'Achat (for the purchase)

Radio Affichage (outdoor) et Television. Carat became so big that the French government, urged by many French ad agencies, banned the brokerage of media and almost put Carat and the media services revolution out of business.

Soon virtually all media in Europe were purchased through media services agencies. The idea spread across the Atlantic. Zenith, the media arm of Saatchi, came to the United States in 1994. In the last five years, every major U.S. ad agency has spun off its media department into a freestanding media services company. Leo Burnett no longer has a media department: Its buying is done through Starcom. The same is true for BBDO and TBWA/Chiat/Day, which use the Omnicom company OMD; Ogilvy's, JWT's, and Y&R's media are planned and bought by Mindshare/MediaEdge.

Now marketers are putting all their creative eggs in one basket when it comes to media planning and buying. Shell-shocked by audiences that have become more powerful and less attentive, marketers are bringing in planners at the start of the creative process instead of handing them already-produced ads to place. Indeed, function now follows form; the choice of media often determines the creative approach.

And what a choice it is! Although the brave new media world has put TV on the defensive, broadcast isn't going dark just yet. In 2006, the six broadcast networks (which include new pledges FOX and its MyNetwork.com and CW, a merger of WB and UPN) and cable still accounted for two out of every three advertising dollars spent in the United States and 38 percent globally. The average American household has a TV set on for 8 hours and 11 minutes a day. And a person at home typically watches it for 4 hours and 32 minutes, according to Nielsen. On any given weeknight, nearly 108 million Americans tune in to the more than 96 channels. Special events draw even bigger numbers: More than 90 million of us saw *Super Bowl XL*. Despite digital recording devices like TiVo and a steady drop in audience sizes, broadcasters have sold between 70 and 80 percent of their prime-time inventory of 15 minutes of commercials an hour. And the most recent upfront buying season ran a very close second to 2005 as the most lucrative ever.

Although it was a very good year for broadcasters, marketers moved

$500 million from broadcast TV and into cable in 2005. More than 80 percent of TV households subscribe to cable or satellite, and broadcasters are witnessing a mass exodus of viewers who are taking their money with them. Soon most TV will be *on-demand*, meaning the viewer pushes a button to order a movie or download a video—27 million Americans are already doing it. TV commercials will be portals to lead viewers to further action on the Net. They'll be able to bookmark an ad to view later, and click an icon during an ad to invite the brand to call or e-mail them. Or they could opt to be whisked to a microsite for deeper information about a product or even a transactional site to buy it.

Today two-thirds of the average media plan is devoted to TV because it's what advertising agencies know and do best. In three years, however, it will be down to half (which is still more than $125 billion). TV seems easier to buy than, say, 20 web sites, but those sites would likely deliver a better return on a marketer's investment. Once they get over their TV bias, ad agencies will start to play the field in earnest—to the tune of $40 billion.

In fact, the whole media landscape will look dramatically different in 2008. Empowered by technology, people will be even more agnostic about, and promiscuous with, their use of and control over media. "Eyeballs"—audience size and raw impressions—used to matter. By 2008, engagement (involvement) will be the metric that matters to marketers. Action will replace watching as the new criterion.

This is marketing to the moment of aperture: offering the right product at the right time before the right prospect instead of trying to break through people's defenses.

Advertising will appear only to those who would be interested. There will be no Pampers pitch to parents long done with diapers and now dealing with college tuition. With the "spray and pray" (think cluster bombs of ads that hopefully hit their targets) era of TV advertising over, wasted circulation will die. Ads in mass media will corral those who are interested in the product or service and drive them to a new location. "Push this button if you're concerned about your cholesterol"; "Press here for a virtual drive of the new Audi." For consumers, this is no longer interruption but relevant information they've requested. For marketers, it's a 100 percent pure audience composition—digital democracy in action. So what can we expect?

In 2005, nearly 70 percent of America's 13,838 radio stations were primarily focused on music. All had 12 to 16 minutes of commercials each hour. In 2008, we'll see a whole lot more, courtesy of satellite and HD.

At one moment in 2005, there were 22,054 magazine titles out there. An average of 29 new ones swell the ranks each month (9 out of 10 quickly fail). In 2008, not only will there be fewer titles on the newsstand but perhaps fewer editors, too. Readers will be able to create their own customized issues digitally and access them on their Treos. We'll build our own digital libraries of favorite articles. Magazines will send us updates about upcoming articles based on topics we've "consumed" before.

The number of daily newspapers (2,372 today) will dwindle. Their print versions will be considerably slimmed as well. No more weekly TV listings or stock pages; those will be readily accessible online. In fact, everything will direct our attention online. The Internet is the world's fastest-growing advertising medium, after all. Some 83 million American households will be online by 2010, with virtually all of them forgoing the telephone modem for broadband (compared with 64 million Net-connected households in 2005 and just 40 million of them using broadband). Computers will link our online search histories to TV viewing patterns to offer us products and services that our past behavior implies we're looking for. Digital budgets that accounted for 5 to 8 percent of the average advertising budgets will soar to 15 to 20 percent. E-mail marketing will rise as consumers opt in to receive content that way. Spam will wither (the people will rejoice).

Since we're TV addicts from way back, the television will still be on. Many five-second "pod puncher" ads will pop up at the end of commercial breaks. Other ads will last for several minutes. Many will mirror a program's theme. More mini-ad pods will appear in news shows, where viewers are more likely to stay tuned through the commercial break to get to the weather report or to a segment that has been promoted.

And the shows and ads that were once linear storytelling will have fewer story arcs and be more of a buffet. We'll take what we want, and then move on. There'll also be more story forming (you affect the outcome) and story dwelling (where a group determines how the story will unfold), just like in videogames (which will be even more realistic and absorbing).

Some of us will be living a second life in these shows, and advertisers will, too. They will plow an estimated $730 million into them by 2010, compared to a mere $56 million in 2005. Personal video recorders, in 10 million American homes in 2005, will be in more than one in every four in 2008. (Nielsen began monitoring them in 2005, and they're now standard on some new TVs.) This means that advertisers will flock to live programming and events like the *Academy Awards*, since dramas and sitcoms are highly TiVoed. Around 90 percent of those who record for later viewing fast-forward through commercials.

Most people will have access to video-on-demand (VOD) content driven by cable and satellite companies, which are pushing it out cheaply. VOD will make content available on everything from portable media players and mobile phones to gaming devices. That means we will watch what we want, when we want, creating our own programming lineup and making the networks' carefully crafted TV lineups no longer "must-see." It won't make the ads ineffective, however: Three out of four consumers don't flip channels once they've activated a VOD program, and 43 percent don't leave the room or multitask while watching.

New media forms like mobisodes, minute-long video segments played on mobile phones, will be commonplace, as will blogs and podcasting. The video offerings that in 2005 were mainly fast-paced, abbreviated, or behind-the-scenes versions of existing TV shows will soon be customized for their screen size. These other video platforms may turn out to be the new, lower-cost pilot system for TV where original shows can be tested.

And what will crop up over and over again on those shows? Branded products, that's what. A PQ Media report from 2006 said that marketers will step up ad creep, placing products wherever they can: in movies, television, and radio shows; on web sites; in video games; in song lyrics; in newspaper and magazine articles; and even in the plots of novels. And while it's not as intense abroad as here, PQ says it's beginning to take off with the EU lifting prohibitions against it. PQ expects spending on paid placements worldwide to jump from $2.2 billion in 2005 to almost $7.6 billion in 2010, led by the United States, Brazil, Australia, France, and Japan.

In Japan, Northwest Airlines now plasters ads on the window-cleaning platforms so workers inside buildings can see them clearly. In Jakarta, Pepsodent turned cleaning gondolas into oversized toothbrushes. Marlboro actually got more efficient and creative after it was forced off TV. Now, in addition to live events it sponsors, and icon-filled lounge areas in bars for its community, it backs an exclusive club where vacationers can relax at a Montana ranch the cigarette-maker owns.

Like at those watering-holes draped in Marlboro pennants, we'll also meet up online. MySpace (or its successor) will be your space in the open-source wiki world. Likeminded folks will create social networks and online neighborhoods will buzz with digital grapevines.

Marketers will expend a lot of energy to get ads or product-related clips e-mailed around that grapevine circuit. Ford's wacky ad on British TV showed the hood of a parked Sportka popping up and knocking out a bird about to perch there. The ad crisscrossed the online world, where it was altered to show a leaping cat getting decapitated by the sunroof. There's no proof, but there is a strong suspicion that Ford's London agency, Ogilvy & Mather, was behind the viral sendup.

DID YOU KNOW:

- Forty-six percent of all magazine and 50 percent of newspaper readers are engaged in some other activity while reading.
- More magazines are read on Mondays and Fridays than any other day.
- More newspapers are read on Sundays and most are read in the morning.
- Magazines are proportionally more often used than any other medium at locations such as doctors' offices and auto repair shops, where people wait for service.
- More people get morning news from TV than from any other news source.

- More TV is watched in January than in any other month, followed by November and February.
- About 19 percent of the time spent with television is also used for eating, housework, and other work.
- Radio is the quintessential background medium: Participants do nothing else but listen to it less than one-third of the time.
- Two-thirds of adults say they multitask while online or while watching TV.
- Forty-one percent of people 18+ say they multitask while reading the newspaper.
- Forty percent of people 18+ say they multitask while reading a magazine.
- The week with Independence Day in it usually has the fewest TV viewers of the year; reruns are in full swing and everyone is outdoors.
- Product placement works best at the start of a program (when fingers come off the fast-forward button) and in live TV like news and sports.
- Sixty-five to 70 percent of mobile devices are used in the home.
- While Saturday night TV has relatively low viewership, those watching tend to be more involved than viewers on other nights.
- The new gadgetry is actually growing the TV audience. Fans who miss an episode of a favorite show often will catch up on an iPod, NBC claims. Others discover shows on their iPod and then tune in to catch them on conventional TV.

When John Wanamaker once complained that he knew that half his advertising budget was wasted, but not *which* half, he gave voice to a conundrum with which marketers have long wrestled. By 2008, marketers will know the answer. Deeper, faster analysis of customer information, thanks to the evolution of data mining and ever-more sophisticated ways to study digital fingerprints, means researchers will know what we want to see and hear even before we do. Advertising will be more of a science and less of an art, and marketing relationships will seem a good deal more intimate.

Feedback will be available in real time, so marketers will be able to adjust pricing and messages on the fly. Marketers will know what commercials work best in certain environments and against certain audiences.

Advertising won't go away: It will go everywhere. And it may become less obvious as it disperses into many messages from more places, directed to different types of people, to tell a story individually customized for each of them. Marketers will no longer see consumers as eaters, players, and viewers but as producers, distributors, marketers, and even partners.

WHAT DOES IT COST?

The average cost of a TV commercial is around $20 per thousand viewers. Typically, a 30-second spot during prime time on a broadcast network costs five times as much as an ad on cable.

In the interactive world, the home page of Yahoo! is typically sold to one advertiser per day. The costs vary on demand, but in general you can expect to reach 25,000,000 individuals in one day. That "unit" costs $255,000 to $425,000.

The home page of MSN is similar: 26,000,000 individuals for approximately $425,000. Otherwise, you are buying a portion of any site's traffic on a cost per thousand (CPM) basis. This ranges from a $3 CPM for very untargeted impressions (number of times an ad banner is downloaded and presumably seen by visitors) to $20 for something more targeted. Certain categories cost upward of $80 to $100 (finance and technology) per thousand.

The following tables compare the rough costs to advertise in a range of familiar media. Do the numbers surprise you?

TV

Average 30-Second Commercial Costs

Program	Network	Cost
Grey's Anatomy	ABC	$212,500
Lost	ABC	$191,250
Desperate Housewives	ABC	$255,000
Monday Night Football	ABC	$255,000
CSI	CBS	$191,250
American Idol	FOX	$340,000
Today Show	NBC	$ 42,500
Tonight Show	NBC	$ 51,000
Novella	Univision	$ 38,250
The Daily Show	Comedy Central	$ 17,000

Magazines

Printed Page (In Color)

Publication	Cost
People	$135,824
Vanity Fair	$ 80,333
Sports Illustrated	$128,683
Essence	$ 48,687
Latina	$ 19,239
Oprah	$ 88,044
Vogue	$ 76,735
GQ	$ 64,838

(Continued)

Billboards

Market	Media Format	People Reached	Cost
New York	Long Island Expressway Bulletin	153,500 daily	$ 91,800
New York	Subway Brand Train	393,120,000 monthly	$140,000
New York	Times Square Bulletin	1.5 million daily	$150,000
New York	Wild Posters (2,500 units)	1,260,000 monthly	$ 20,043
New York	Men's Restroom Displays (248 units)	1,980,000 monthly	$ 6,375
Chicago	King-Size Bus Posters (#25 showing, 250 units)	28,557,500 monthly	$ 78,750
Chicago	Kennedy Expressway Bulletin	194,500 daily	$ 42,500
Chicago	Dan Ryan Expressway Bulletin	214,760 daily	$ 12,750
Chicago	Healthclub Panels (56 units)	1,141,209 monthly	$ 18,670
Boston	Bus Shelters (25 units)	n/a	$ 49,215
Boston	Mass Pike Wall	150,000 daily	$ 22,950
San Francisco	Commuter Rail Two-Sheet Platform Posters (100 units)	17,780,000 monthly	$ 30,000
Philadelphia	Commuter Rail Two-Sheet Platform Posters (104 units)	2,385,840 monthly	$ 21,215
Philadelphia	Healthclub Panels (16 units)	960,000 monthly	$ 5,848

Newspapers and Radio

Newspaper, Black & White Page	Cost
Wall Street Journal	$70,162
New York Times, daily cost	$47,322
New York Times, Sunday cost	$72,317

Radio	Cost
30-second national radio spot on Rush Limbaugh	$ 4,420
30-second national radio spot on Ryan Seacrest	$ 1,615

2

WHAT *REVELATIONS* REVEALED . . . AND *NARNIA* CONFIRMED

In April 2005, it seemed like a religious revival was sweeping the country. All that was missing was a snake-handler reality show. Mel Gibson's *The Passion of the Christ* had generated more than $600 million at the box-office. Dan Brown's *Da Vinci Code* held its perch on best-seller lists for two years and counting. More than 62 million copies of the *Left Behind* thrillers (based on a literal interpretation of the Revelation) had been snapped up and the thirteenth novel in the series had just hit book-stores. Terri Schiavo, who'd languished in a vegetative state, finally died (although the scalding debate about pulling the plug on her had not). Huge audiences tuned in to watch the funeral of Pope John Paul II with all its solemn pageantry, barely two weeks before. NBC, stuck in fourth place in the rankings and unable to command the advertising rates of its rivals, thought it had found the miracle it desperately needed: a big-budget, six-week, eerie miniseries, *Revelations*, about the coming Apoca-lypse—the ultimate clash between Christ and Satan as painted in the final book of the New Testament. They promoted it widely as "Apocalypse Wow" and unveiled it during May sweeps.

Trying to squelch NBC's faith, Fox offered another idol to worship that night. It expanded its top-rated *American Idol* results show to a full hour and pulled in a hefty 25 million viewers. Still, 15.5 million tuned in for the first hour of *Revelations*, and almost 12 million returned a week later for the second installment. It wasn't just the size of the prime-time congregation that boded well (a bigger group than those who'd watched any original episode of *The West Wing* in that same time period that *Revelations* temporarily occupied), it was their demography: young and moneyed.

But there was little euphoria in NBC's war rooms. Mixing pixels and prophecy is risky. America is a deeply religious country. In a May 2005 Gallup poll, 42 percent of the populace—some 80 million people—identify themselves as born-again or evangelical Christians. Three out of five consider faith a high personal priority, and more attend a religious service of some kind every week than go to all sporting events combined.

Religion (or at least contemporary executions of it) and TV make for an explosive cocktail. When *Revelations* producers Gavin Polone (*Panic Room*) and David Seltzer (*The Omen*) initially pitched the concept to the networks, a few rejected it outright because of the subject matter. Religion, Seltzer has said, is "one of TV's most heavily fortified taboos."

It is fortified because advertisers are notoriously antsy about running their commercials on a show viewers might decide is controversial. In the United States, religion polarizes and evokes more controversy than any other subject. Advertisers know that and it's advertisers who control the strings in the traditional media industry. They withheld ad support and made *Revelations* a charity-case for NBC.

Volkswagen had an option to buy and passed. So did KFC and General Motors. NBC could not fill its dance card, let alone get the $221,000 for a 30-second spot it wanted. (That was a tad pricier than the average cost for a similar spot on *The West Wing*, but less than that for its hospital drama *ER*.) It settled for less all around.

Even though three levels of fact-checkers pored over *Revelations* and a religious adviser gave it final approval, the series still antagonized the Religious Right for being what they considered religiously wrong. They blasted the show for biblical illiteracy in the way it treated the scriptures and glamorized the occult. *Left Behind* co-author Jerry Jenkins called it "a mishmash of myth, silliness and misrepresentations of scripture." Ted Haggard, president of the National Association of Evangelicals, dismissed it as "one more attempt by non-believing liberals to interpret sacred texts" and in the process, "make fools of themselves."

Then there was the graphic violence. The opening montage features violent images of civil wars in Africa and a man plummeting from a skyscraper. In the first episode, skeptic and Harvard astrophysicist Richard Massey's teen daughter is abducted and killed by a Satanist and has her heart ripped out. Massey, played by Bill Pullman, tracks down the girl's murderer and teams with a nun, Sister Josepha Montafiore (actress Natascha McElhone) at the hospital bed of a brain-dead girl who inexplicably begins uttering Latin scriptures and who, it is suggested, may be connected to Massey's daughter. Meanwhile, a ship disaster in the Adriatic yielded one survivor: a baby who mysteriously might be connected to God or Satan.

It makes a few colorful swear-words or a Three Stoogesesque smack on the head seem like Saturday morning kidstuff. But 30 years ago, that's all it took to fire up Methodist minister Donald Wildmon. One night in pre-cable 1977, Wildmon watched TV with his family and was disgusted to find adultery on one channel, cursing on the next, and a man beating another man with a hammer on the third. That set him off: He touted "Turn Off the TV Week" at his church and issued a press release that reeled the media in. That led to his founding the Mississippi-based National Federation for Decency advocacy group, which was renamed the American Family Association in 1988 and became a force to be reckoned with.

When it first aired in 1993, *N.Y.P.D. Blue* faced the American Family Association, which castigated ABC for the show's then-unusual use of profanity, violence, and nudity. Sometimes too much attention is as bad as not enough. With that kind of intimidation from grassroots movements, marketers bail. As a result of the controversy stirred up by the AFA, most episodes that first year were so advertising-light that ABC asked the producers to tack on several minutes of the actual show to make up for the advertising shortfall. And most of the advertisers who were there were B stringers—brands like Cortizone-10 anti-itch ointment, Permathene-12 diet aid, and Wash 'n Curl shampoo. Only after months of critical acclaim and growing audience interest did mainstream advertisers come aboard.

More often, they let the show go. In 2003, CBS couldn't withstand right-wing complaints about *The Reagans*, so that show got booted to cable. The networks got cold feet over *Angels in America*, a movie about AIDS, so it ran on HBO. In April 2005, when the American Family Association objected to a *Will & Grace* episode set to air the Thursday before Good Friday that seemed to mock Christ's crucifixion, NBC scrambled to explain that its own press release was mistaken—that the episode had not even been finalized.

In May 12, 2006, General Motors (GM) announced it was expanding its advertising relationship with the huge hit *Survivor*. The car maker had sponsored the reality show since it debuted on CBS in July 2000, and in spring 2006 had accounted for a fifth of the show's advertising revenue.

Less than three months later, GM pulled out of the show's next season completely, denying it had anything to do with the controversial plan to divide competing teams based on race—or the criticism heaped on it for that. Other advertisers from previous seasons also got off the island, including Coca-Cola, Home Depot, United Parcel Service, and Campbell Soup.

Many marketers resisted right-wing indignation and parked on Wisteria Lane. The audience for *Desperate Housewives* is so massive (more than 20 million) and established that it's hard for advertisers not to heed this siren call.

The two-hour premiere of *The Book of Daniel* in January 2005 had only 23 national commercials spanning 12½ minutes (plus promos and public service announcements), about half the usual inventory for network prime time. Combe Inc. bought 30 seconds at a bargain rate to promote Just for Men. The 10 P.M. drama revolved around a modern Episcopal priest addicted to Vicodin, whose wife drinks and teen daughter peddles pot, whose 23-year-old son is gay, and whose adopted Chinese son is sleeping with the teenage daughter of one of the church's most upright benefactors. His brother-in-law may have absconded with the millions raised to build a new church school. The priest, Daniel Webster, regularly discusses his dysfunctional clan with Jesus, who comes across as a nebbish.

Daniel was fashioned to attract the right demographic—young, educated, affluent—viewers who like their TV edgy. A *King Kong* commercial in the premiere stretched two and a half minutes. But *Daniel* also attracted censure from the American Family Association for its "anti-Christian" aura, prompting five of NBC's 232 affiliates to preempt the series. The WB affiliate in Little Rock, Arkansas, ran it when the local NBC affiliate balked. By the second episode, after AFA congregants called the Just for Men client, Combe Inc., to protest, it disappeared faster than those stubborn gray hairs it promised to dye. After week four, so had *Daniel*.

Evangelical zeal motivated marketers like Coca-Cola, Pine-Sol, Chevrolet, and Bank of America to put money behind efforts to woo this family-focused, brand-loyal market by sponsoring church events. But it has put other marketers on the defensive. Toyota and Gateway scurried away from FX's plastic surgery drama *Nip/Tuck* after the Parents Television Council sent around racy rundowns from the show and lambasted it as "one of the most sexually explicit, profane and violent programs in the history of American television." Lowe's apologized for calling evergreens "holiday" rather than "Christmas" trees. Target pledged to "become more specific to the holiday Christmas and Hanukkah holiday" when the American Family Association threatened boycott.

In 1990, Phil Guarascio, the then head of media services at General Motors, actually went to Tupelo, Mississippi to meet with Wildmon and learn what makes the AFA tick—and what gets them ticked off. After all, the Bible Belt buys a lot of GM cars, particularly those high-profit margin pickups. Guarascio found that the reverend had a system: 500 women armed with score sheets decided what content was objectionable enough that an ad shouldn't appear next to it. GM used the score sheet as a key to avoid landing in AFA's crosshairs.

Saturn appealed to a different market: the well-educated, coastal, recreational cyclist crowd. Saturn's agency, Hal Riney & Partners, had gotten the brand team to approve a schedule in *Playboy*. The insertion order was already out when GM pulled the plug in fear of Wildmon.

Although it can be vociferous, the AFA isn't always persuasive. When it tried to press Procter & Gamble Co. (P&G) to pull out of NBC's *Will & Grace* and Bravo's *Queer Eye for the Straight Guy*, P&G held firm. When P&G was absent it contended that it had not changed its media buys under external pressure but was only on the sidelines when the content didn't fit its guidelines or because there was no inventory available.

But even if advocacy groups don't bring advertisers to their knees, the prospect of finding themselves in a negative limelight can make even the most lion-hearted cringe. None of them wants to look like it is rolling over on an issue of principle, but at the same time, none wants to antagonize any of its customers. After AFA threatened to boycott Ford for purportedly supporting "the homosexual agenda," the car company promised to stop advertising in gay publications. When that decision elicited a public outcry from the other side, Ford reversed itself.

In 2001, soon after Carat won a big Fortune 100 account, its CEO received a number of letters complaining about a show the company had sponsored. Being new to TV, the CEO called me in to say how unhappy he was about the letters. I should have known better, since this was a company that avoids *Redbook* and *Cosmo* because they're too sexy. I tried to explain that this was a pretty typical occurrence and that a sponsor needs to evaluate how many negative comments it receives and how vitriolic they were. The CEO cut me off. "I don't want to receive one more letter," he said flatly. That led to Carat setting up a prescreen unit for everything this client touches.

There's very little media guys like me don't see ahead of time. *Saturday Night Live* should really be *Friday Night Live* because advertisers see the skits in a dress rehearsal to make sure the content is not objectionable. And just as there are self-triggering ads—the temperature drops below 32 degrees and a Campbell Soup spot gets the green flag, and when the pollen count is high, Zyrtec ads can roll—they also have a degree of disaster control in the airplane-crash policy. All contracts with airline accounts stipulate that when a plane goes down, all aviation ads go down with it. This kind of automatic pull will be showing up more and more in other industries with their related crises.

Sometimes, the power-brokering line between cause and effect is serpentine. In 2005, Stephen Wright and his gay life partner, John Wright, trumped six other nonmainstream families—one African-American, another Hispanic, a third Korean, and so on—to win a four-bedroom, red-brick McMansion on a cul-de-sac in the Circle C Ranch development in Austin, Texas. The Wrights had persuaded the overwhelmingly white, Christian, Republican neighbors to want them next door. ABC had heavily promoted *Welcome to the Neighborhood* and slotted the unscripted series as a summer replacement for *Desperate Housewives*. Ten days before its intended debut, ABC canned it. Their explanation: Viewers might object to the early homophobic barbs that in time would give way to open-minded acceptance. But the real reason for it being canned, contended co-producers Bill and Eric Kennedy, actually had to do with a different show altogether, *The Chronicles of Narnia: The Lion, the Witch and the Wardrobe*. ABC parent Disney had carefully wooed the Evangelical community to see the C. S. Lewis faith-centric film. Four religious groups, including the Southern Baptist Convention's more than 16 million members, had recently lifted longtime boycotts against Disney (ignited for its supposedly pro-gay attitudes) and no one at ABC and Disney wanted to rock the pro-Christian boat again. Very quickly, *Narnia* earned back its huge investment many times over.

With so many other media options tantalizing its audience, network TV has been forced to do "feature television" that relies on special effects and big-name movie stars (think Jerry Bruckheimer's *CSI* on CBS). Advertisers like the swagger and style of these big movies, but their reluctance to take risks means that a show with controversial content and a definite point of view is rare.

3

WHY ADVERTISERS HAVE STOPPED LAUGHING AT SITCOMS

When *Friends* ended its 10-year run on NBC on May 6, 2004, it was not because the sitcom had grown as stale as the show's theme song by The Rembrandts or as old as the 40-year-old Courteney Cox and Lisa Kudrow playing young thirtysomethings who began as twentysomethings when the show debuted. Nor did the "must-see" show end because the ratings had plummeted. Sure, the ratings had softened, but they were still the kind of numbers that make a network's night. It was still "must-see TV." No, the popular sitcom faded into increased syndication because the six main actors and the production company—grown fat on this cash cow—wanted out.

Advertisers liked who was watching—young, upscale, monied—and paid dearly to reach them. *Friends* was long the most expensive show on TV. In November 2003, the average 30-second spot on it cost $473,500, compared to $310,324 for *CSI*, $237,000 for *Apprentice*, and $197,050 for 30 seconds on *Law & Order*. And when 52.25 million viewers tuned in to the two-hour finale (actually, 66 minutes), advertisers forked over $2 million for half a minute. And why shouldn't they? Advertisers had only seen sitcom numbers like these three other times, with the series finales of

M*A*S*H (106 million), *Cheers* (80.4 million), and *Seinfeld* (76.3 million). Throughout its run, *Friends* defined "appointment TV."

But appointment TV and perhaps even sitcoms themselves seem strangely anachronistic in these times. In this on-demand economy, with so many cable channels targeting specific interests and so many ways to summon one's entertainment, viewers are in control of what they see and when they see it. It may still resonate with older folks (yes, we're talking to you 40-year-olds born in the 1960s) who grew up watching "must-see TV" on Thursday nights. Appointment TV meant we tuned in on Monday night for football or stayed home on Saturday night for *The Love Boat*, or finished our Wednesday night workout before *Law & Order* began at 10 P.M. Appointment TV on Thursday night is traditionally the most prized by advertisers for its ability to influence viewers' purchases on their upcoming weekends, but for the young today, appointment TV is as meaningless as the growing acronyms of L&WSVUCITBJ (That's *Law & Order Special Victims Unit, Criminal Intent* and the now-canceled *Trial By Jury*).

This is certainly nothing to laugh about if you are the head of programming for NBC, but it's even worse if you are producing sitcoms. Even the *format* of sitcoms feels tired—the lighting, the costuming, the laugh track, a story arc that plays out like a soap opera, the two or three stories happening concurrently in the show, the end-of-season cliffhanger and the resolution in the same episode. In many current hits like Fox's *Prison Break* and *24*, the plot extends over many episodes or even the entire season. In *24*, each episode unfolds in real time representing one hour in the life of our protagonist, counterterrorist agent Jack Bauer, played by Keifer Sutherland.

It's gotten so bad that even good sitcoms such as *Arrested Development* are canceled after three seasons of low ratings. There was even a sitcom pilot about how bad sitcoms have become. Entitled *Nobody's Watching*, this sitcom pilot opens with these visionary words of warning:

> This is a message for all of you TV networks. Lately your sitcoms suck. *They Suck!*

While it might be hyperbole, it's not unfair to say that nobody's watching sitcoms on television. In fact, we all know this because the smart writers of *Nobody's Watching* posted their pilot at YouTube.com on that great postmodern TV network called the Internet where more than 500,000 people have watched it. According to news reports, NBC has now picked up *Nobody's Watching* for development. Not for Thursday night, though; no, NBC wants it for its online broadband channel.

If sitcoms seem so yesterday, it could be because that's when they began. Sitcoms are as old as TV itself—even older, as they thrived on radio before. But the first genuine blockbusting tone-setter debuted in 1951. Every producer to whom he'd shopped the concept turned him down, so a thick-accented Cuban bandleader and his perky red-headed wife put together a sitcom of their own. The success of *I Love Lucy* spawned a bevy of other sitcoms, such as *Ozzie and Harriet*, *Make Room for Daddy*, *My Three Sons*, *The Beverly Hillbillies*, *The Mary Tyler Moore Show*, and *Bewitched*. By 1952, for the first time, the number of sitcoms on TV equaled the number of comedy-variety shows (22 each). By the 1962–63 season, there were 30 sitcoms on air, and by the 1979-80 season, there were 45 shows, representing half of what was then on prime time.

There were, of course, many situation comedy hits after that—*Cheers*, *Family Ties*, *Newhart*, *The Cosby Show*, *M*A*S*H* (when that ended after 11 years, 77 percent of all televisions turned on were tuned to it)—but the genre began an inexorable decline.

By the end of the 2003-04 TV season, it was *Survivor* that went head to head against *Friends* . . . . and survived. For the first time in 18 years, thanks to *Survivor* and its forensics drama, *CSI*, CBS had more total viewers on Thursday night than NBC. Once scorned as the "geezer network," it had also dominated among 18-to-49-year-olds, the alpha demographic for marketers.

Sitcoms had ceded their halos and, like made-for-TV movies, miniseries, and newsmagazines, were on the wane. Even one drama, which typically runs an hour, was easier to develop than two half-hour sitcoms. Not even the *Friends* spin-off, *Joey*, could gel with viewers or advertisers. TV's new idol was, and is, *American Idol*, the top-rated TV show in the United States and, in fact, the entire reality genre.

At first, advertisers sniffed at the questionable content of these unscripted shows, but as they almost doubled ratings virtually overnight, they quickly relented. And surprisingly, their content is relatively chaste next to sitcoms. Networks were elated. Reality shows are relatively cheap to produce ($150,000 vs. $1 million or more for a half-hour sitcom) and they seed much faster than dramas with one big star—which traditionally build faster than sitcoms with ensembles. *The Apprentice* upended the theory that reality TV audiences are largely downscale. And products could be showcased easily and integrated into the show. That's why in TV alley they call reality shows "network crack."

NBC, with its inability to attract enough viewers with sitcoms and the *Law & Order* franchise, succumbed to its own stash of this crack in the form of the gory *Fear Factor*, with its animal testicle-eating and alligator-wrestling stunt-contests, The Donald's *Apprentice*, and the *Deal or No Deal* game show, which in the spring of 2006 attracted more viewers than any series in its time block in nine years—more than watched the NCAA championship basketball game on CBS or 24 on Fox at the same time.

Even Steven Spielberg, the master of scripted fare, has been seduced. He joined with Mark Burnett, who produced the mega-reality-hits, to create an *American Idol*–like contest-show to find the nation's next great filmmaker. Home viewers of the (now proposed) *On the Lot* series vote on which aspiring director makes it to the next round each week and ultimately lands a Hollywood development deal at DreamWorks.

In 1995, marketers paid a premium to run their ads on sitcoms. While we know this to be true from our own experience in the advertising business, it was validated by an FCC media bureau staff research paper with the very serious-sounding name, "Empirical Aspects of Advertiser Preferences and Program Content of Network TV." The research concluded that advertisers paid less for news and police programs because they were viewed as darker and more unfriendly milieus for ads. The theory was that lighter programming puts viewers in a more receptive mood for ads.

New research, new metrics, and new thinking stand this conclusion on its head and appear to whack another nail into the sitcom coffin. Marketers are now interested in a program's relevance to its audience—whether they "lean toward" the TV or "lean back" while watching it. It seems that viewers remember ads in news shows or other programs where they're watching purposefully, much better than they recall ads in entertainment shows. If they need to watch a program for work, school, travel, or just to remain part of their social network, they are more attentive to the ads.

If you want further evidence that advertisers have stopped laughing at sitcoms, just look at ABC's prime-time schedule for fall 2006. The entire prime-time schedule features only two new sitcoms—that's right, *two!*

Back in the heady days of ABC's Friday-night TGIF (Thank Goodness It's Funny), the network had four sitcoms just on Friday night alone. This was appointment TV for families, a less-attractive cousin of NBC's must-see Thursday-night two-hour block of comedies. It even had its own logo. However, in 2006, on ABC, a dancing Jerry Springer racked up higher ratings than Ted Danson's new sitcom for the network.

But perhaps the principal reason why advertisers aren't laughing at sitcoms any longer is because media power has gone to the people. TiVo, while not the phenomenal success that was once predicted, represents the forefront of what's coming—which is citizen editors. Digital video recorders (DVRs), now in just 8 percent of American homes, should be in 40 percent by 2009. The lessons to take away from this are that users are far likelier to TiVo weekly dramas and sitcoms and not TiVo live sports and events such as the *Academy Awards, Olympics, Super Bowl* and *Grammys,* which they want to watch as they happen—and that around 90 percent of the time when people TiVo a show, they fast-forward through the ads. It's not hard to see why advertisers want to shirk shows that are the most likely to be TiVoed.

And video-on-demand from cable companies (which have been largely giving it away for free to build loyalty) is mushrooming. In 2005, subscribers of Comcast, the nation's largest cable company, watched 1.4 billion programs on demand. That's twice as many as they saw in 2004. Consulting firm Accenture figures that ad skipping and on-demand viewing could cost the TV industry $27 billion in lost advertising revenue by 2010.

The networks, seeking to make up some of that potential outflow, have turned to consumers (rather than advertisers) for recompense. (After all, people don't seem to object to shelling out for ring-tones or satellite radio.) DirecTV customers can download an ad-free NBC prime-time show for 99 cents and iTunes customers can download an ad-free episode of *Desperate Housewives* from ABC the day after it airs for $1.99. Comcast customers can watch CBS hits via video-on-demand but currently they're offered ad-intact.

However, until TV producers can figure out what do with these humorous online videos in prime-time, the closest thing to YouTube.com on television is Al Gore's *Current TV*. On August 1, 2005, the former U.S. vice president and his partner, Joe Hyatt, a lawyer, entrepreneur, and business professor at Stanford, launched a new television channel with a new model. In the 400-channel pack, it's the only 24-hour network based around viewer-created content. Targeted at young people, the *Current* TV Network was designed to "fight the tyranny of the mass media" where content is dished out. At *Current*, it's dished in.

Young mediagrazers using inexpensive home video cameras and video editing software create the content (they call it VC^2 or VC-squared), which is in the form of videopods anywhere from one to seven minutes long. (Full disclosure: To get things going, pros did most of it in the beginning.) In this video-smorgasbord you could find the inspired and the insipid: anything from a piece about the emotional trauma that the Israeli troops underwent when removing the Jewish settlers from Gaza, to a mockumentary about a pizza-delivery boy, replete with fart jokes, to profiles of a Romanian Internet sex worker, a hang glider, a fish-market worker, and Jesse Billauer, a Malibu surfer-turned-quadriplegic-turned-surfer-again. A timer in the corner of the screen shows how much of that particular segment is left to run.

Critics have likened the minicapsules to tasty appetizers. Compared to them, an hour-long drama seems like a five-course meal. Gore has called them democratic (with a small *d*) presentations "by the people, for the people." That the people yearn to sound off—and to listen to themselves—demonstrates we're a nation, if not a world, of grassroots story-tellers. That's why at a recent moment in time—July 31, 2006—based on Technocrati's index there were 50 million blogs in the blogosphere with 175,000 new ones starting every day. More about blogs later; the point here is that *Current TV* tapped into the next great wave, one that like a tsunami may someday soon wash reality shows off TV's stage.

It's not just journalism affected by citizen media. It's advertising itself. After a spot created by a 19-year-old Minneapolis man showing Sony gizmos transforming—a stereo morphs into a TV, which becomes a DVD player, a laptop, a digital camera, and then the Sony logo—traveled the Web to acclaim, *Current* posted the animator's spot and Sony paid to run it. Toyota and L'Oreal also have deals to run consumer-generated spots on *Current*.

JetBlue, Converse, MasterCard, and Chrysler have also employed user-generated content to connect with Internet-savvy young people. On priceless.com, consumers were invited to provide copy to already-shot visuals, and more than 1,500 homemade commercials were submitted to conversegallery.com. Converse ran some of the best on TV.

Of course, when marketers recognize that they are no longer brand guardians, but rather brand hosts, and cede control, things can go awry. Chevrolet learned that painful lesson in March 2006. It invited visitors to chevyapprentice.com (after the show had focused on marketing the 2007 Tahoe) to use the video clips and music provided to make their own ad for the SUV. In one ad, a shiny Tahoe winds down a country road lined with sunflower fields. Then the script appears: "$70 to fill up the tank, which will last less than 400 miles. Chevy Tahoe." Another pictured the SUV in the desert: "Our planet's oil is almost gone. . . . You don't need GPS to see where this road leads." Or "Like this snowy wilderness? Better get your fill of it now. Then say hello to global warming."

You get the picture. Chevy had hoped to seed a viral e-mail campaign for its coolness but instead got brickbats for its environmental unfriendliness. A prominently played piece in *The New York Times* (among many other pieces) ran the contest off-road. Of 30 ads posted on YouTube.com, almost all were anti-Tahoe. To its credit, Chevy acknowledged that the results were an inevitable part of playing in this space and handing the keys to the people.

The truth is that even if Chevy hadn't left the keys in the engine with a full tank of gas, the people would have found a way to break in. And more and more, they will. Their power to go where they want to go makes appointment TV less commanding. And it makes sitcoms a lot less funny.

4

WHY RATINGS ARE OVERRATED: THE WEIRDNESS OF SWEEPS, A. C. NIELSEN, AND THE UPFRONT

On May 4, 2005, ABC went gunning for Paula Abdul, one of the three judges of Fox's powerhouse talent show, *American Idol*.

In ABC's hour-long *Primetime Live* special, dubbed "Fallen Idol," an itinerant 22-year-old former contestant, Corey Clark, revealed that 1980s pop diva and *Idol* judge Paula Abdul had illicitly coached him through his singing and dancing on the show and his performance in other areas as well. He presented purported evidence of their tryst: tapes of Abdul warning him to stay mum about their relationship, a bottle of cough syrup prescribed to her that he claimed she'd given him, phone logs documenting frequent contact, Clark's familiarity with Abdul's three dogs, the revelation that Abdul instructed him to sing a song that Randy Jackson had once performed, and Clark's parents' collaboration of their son's testimony. On the news show, other contestants complained they did not get the same help and preferential treatment as Clark.

The boy toy's motives were unambiguous: He was, after all, shopping for a publisher for his "famewhore" kiss-'n'-tell e-book and got to perform portions of his tell-all song, "Paulatics," from the album he was recording:

> Your possibilities have gone to the top
> And if you breathe a word you will be dropped
> Your personality at first seemed to be so sweet
> But then I saw the you that they'll never show on TV.

Primetime Live's objective was equally crystalline. It was the month of May. The show, like many on television, was struggling for May ratings. It was fighting to stay on the air. Like Corey, ABC had skin in the game that May as well. So, ABC aired the story in May. It moved this dirty laundry of sex, lies, and videotape from its regular May time slot on the schedule to face *Idol*'s results show during that first week in May.

Oh, and did we mention that it was May?

Yes, young Corey's tell-all on ABC did not air during any random week, but during the all-important sweeps. Dictionary.com gives 14 meanings for the noun *sweeps*. Number 13 is all about television ratings:

a. The period each fall, winter, and spring when television ratings are accrued and studied and advertising rates are reset (the established sweeps periods are November, February and May).
b. The national survey of local stations that is conducted to determine these ratings.

Sweeps began in 1950, when the A. C. Nielsen Co. mailed out paper diaries to a smattering of residents across the country to record what they watched with pen or pencil. It would be too expensive to tally everyone in America, so Nielsen decided to extrapolate year-round viewing numbers from four surveys done annually. These were collected "sweeping" from the Northeast across the land, giving the TV and marketing industries the first ratings on which to base advertising prices for television commercials. Over time, the term *sweeps* entered the English lexicon.

Once television executives and local station managers realized that the results from those four time periods determined what they could charge for the next three months, they took to spectacular gimmicks to attract viewers—and went into overdrive hyping these gimmicks.

In May 2005, ABC "played the press like a Strad," promising to explore "explosive claims about behind-the-scenes activities" at TV's top-rated show and withholding tapes normally sent to critics beforehand, remarked *Philadelphia Inquirer* TV critic Gail Shister.

The ends seemed to justify the meanness. *Primetime Live* did steal some of *Idol's* thunder. On average, *Idol* had been pulling in 28 million viewers each episode and had propelled Fox from fourth to first place among 18- to 49-year-olds, the demographic it most prizes. With "Fallen Idol," *Primetime Live* tapped into this huge audience and got twice its normal viewership (13.8 million), giving ABC its first-ever victory in the 10 P.M. time slot across all demographics. Among adults 18 to 49, it recorded a 144 percent jump above its season average.

During sweeps, making hay with *Idol* "was much too delicious for ABC to pass up," Steve Friedman, former executive producer at NBC's *Today Show* and CBS's *Early Show*, remarked on CNN. *Washington Post* reporter Sally Quinn chimed in: "Nothing matters but ratings. I don't care whether you have a journalism show or not; if you are going to get the ratings, that really is the bottom line."

Why are ratings overrated?

It's because sweeps are more gimmick than gravitas. To get to a bigger bottom line, networks have pulled out a variety of shenanigans, cliffhangers, reunions, guest-stars, events, and exclusives. In November 2005, NBC broadcast *Medium* in 3-D with a *TV Guide* insert providing the glasses so viewers could better see the psychic visions of Patricia Arquette's character. In its *Las Vegas* finale, the pencil-thin Lara Flynn Boyle's character was blown off a roof by high winds and died. Earlier, Barry Bostwick (forever "Brad" in *The Rocky Horror Picture Show* in 1975), guest-starred as a deranged serial killer about to be released from prison unless CBS's *Cold Case* crew could pin an old unsolved murder on him. And in 2004, ABC upped the *Who Wants to Be a Millionaire* ante by paying out 10 million dollars in a "Super Millionaire" sweeps stunt.

The local stations themselves have also poured on the sensationalism with segments like "Salad Bars That Kill," and "Can a Tsunami Happen Here?" Fred Powers, a reporter at CBS's Atlanta affiliate WGCL-TV, was shot three times (unharmed because he was wearing a bulletproof vest) in a live SWAT-team demonstration and was jolted with 50,000 volts from a stun gun that the Georgia State Patrol was about to distribute to its officers.

And in probably one of the most nakedly sweeping gimmicks of all time, Cleveland viewers saw WOIO-TV news anchor Sharon Reed pose nude for the cameras. In fact, to fully appreciate just how naked their motives were, read how the story was promoted and introduced by Sharon's co-anchor:

> What do you get when you combine a beautiful Saturday morning, a Downtown Cleveland venue, a world-famous photographer and over a thousand Clevelanders . . . completely naked?
>
> How about art?
>
> It all happened recently, and 19 Action News anchor Sharon Reed was there.
>
> But Sharon didn't just report the story, she became part of it—posing nude with over a thousand others for a groundbreaking and controversial photo that all of Cleveland will be talking about. . . . It was the latest installation by artist Spencer Tunick!
>
> Our cameras were rolling as the unbelievable scene took place.
>
> Is it art? Or is it something else? You decide.

We'll let you check out Spencer's web site to decide if it's art, but we can promise you that WOIO's story was "something else." It was a sweeps gimmick and, as you might expect, the broadcast drew a record 700,000 viewers. If you need evidence beyond the fact that they picked WOIO's hottest and best-looking anchor to "cover" the story, we should also note that the public nudity event had actually taken place five months before it aired and was held specifically to improve ratings during the all-important sweeps.

Here's the point: If I'm buying billions of dollars in television commercial time (which Carat does), why should the price I pay be based on the night when the news anchor in Cleveland is naked or *Primetime Live* is bashing Paula Abdul or the women of *Desperate Housewives* are on for two hours instead of their usual one? That would be basing advertising rates on an inflated gimmick rather than on average viewership over time. Ratings are overrated because *sweeps* makes them overrated!

Sweeps, after all, sets the rates for local advertisers in TV markets as big as New York City with its more than seven million TV households and as small as the 15,480 in North Platte, Nebraska. Nearly $22.5 billion in local advertising is up for grabs annually. Nielsen combines who watched what and when (by quarter-hours) from the diaries, with automatic reads of what's playing when from its meters in larger markets (relayed via modem early in the morning to Nielsen's central computers) to project daily viewing data.

The two most important things to remember about Nielsen are ratings and shares:

> **Ratings:** One ratings point represents 1 percent (1,102,139) of the 110,213,139 households in America with a television. On cable television, executives and advertisers get excited about anything over 3 points (or 3 million viewers). On broadcast television, the top shows earn between 15 and 25 points (or 15 to 25 million viewers).
>
> **Shares:** This is measured in the percentage of television sets tuned in to a show. So, if the original *CSI* earned a 7 share, then 7 percent of households watching television at 9 P.M. on Thursday night were tuned in.

Founded in 1923 to measure audiences for the then-nascent radio industry, Nielsen produces the currency around which the advertising and TV industries rotate. It provides the average audience tuned to virtually every program on the air during an average minute via 22,400 diaries and 5,100 paperback-book-sized boxes called People Meters in the 56 largest U.S. markets. The number fluctuates some as a few hundred Nielsen households enter and exit each month. Nielsen likes to say that even though its sample is relatively small, it's "well stirred" to represent the nation's diversity in exact proportion. For example, 11 to 12 percent of its panel members are African American—the same as in the overall population.

Nielsen's tallies are used to set ad rates on a cost per thousand (CPM) basis. However, because Neilsen also tells advertisers the demographics of who is watching, the numbers that most resonate with marketers are how a show fares with those 18- to 49-year-olds. A 2.7 share in this key demographic means that 2.7 percent of Americans aged 18 to 49 (who also had their television set turned on) watched this episode—and that can be as many as 100 million 18- to 49-year-olds.

Advertisers buy *cumulative* or *gross rating* points. So, if a TV commercial runs on a show with a 20 rating, that 20 rating would be one integer. Add in the ratings from all the other shows that the marketer bought and the total would comprise the gross rating points. Some advertisers buy widely when looking for reach, perhaps being seen by 90 percent of those watching TV, while others buy big on shows with huge ratings and shares—such as the *Super Bowl.*

All of this sounds well and good until you understand that even with the tiniest fraction of a rating point translating into vast caches of currency, marketers haven't a clue as to how many viewers are actually watching from the household where the set is on—or even whether their message is beaming to an empty room.

If you want to understand why ratings are overrated, just ask yourself if you've ever left your television on while you've actually been doing something else in another part of the house. In fact, there is a long-simmering dissatisfaction with—and distrust of—audience measurement ratings, and this dissatisfaction has gotten louder lately because of the availability of better ratings from other media—and from other countries. For example, advertisers pay only when a searcher clicks on its online ad. The metrics provided by online media companies such as Google, AOL, Yahoo! and others is vastly more helpful to advertisers than what is provided by Nielsen. And in other developed countries around the world, rating services can tell minute by minute *who* is watching the ads.

Assaulted by the comparison, the TV measurement system is evolving both in what it tracks, and how it tracks it. Since December 2005, Nielsen has been following (1) viewers watching when programs initially air (called "live ratings"); (2) live viewers *and* those who play back a show on a DVR the same day that it aired ("live and same-day ratings"), and (3) live viewers and those who play back programs on DVRs within a week of broadcast ("live plus seven-day ratings"). Advertisers contend that roughly four out of five people who record a program to watch later edit out the ads. While DVRs aren't widespread in America's dens yet (only 11 percent in 2006), one in five homes should have them by 2008, and 40 percent by 2010, according to predictions of researcher In-Stat.

Most media buyers growl that they should pay only for "live" viewing. The networks, on the other hand, want to charge based on the total number of viewers, including those who'll tape a show to see later. (In 2006, ABC went so far as to try to refuse to negotiate with those who won't buy total audiences.) The networks even contend that DVR owners are actually more attentive to ads than "live" viewers, who may leave or zone out during the commercial breaks.

Nielsen's diaries were unreliable to the extent that respondents filled them out, not immediately after they watched something but days later. Then they often remembered faultily, exaggerated their loyalty to a beloved show, lazily filled in that they watched *The Today Show* every morning instead of three times a week, or outright lied to buff their image (hence CNN vs. The Cartoon Network). The 1.6 million handwritten diaries are slowly being supplemented—and possibly supplanted—by electronic People Meters attached to TVs, satellite dishes, and so on. The ratings generated by the two approaches rarely coincide, leading beneficiaries to praise the more accurate devices, victims to decry them, and advertisers to press for rate concessions.

People Meters, which still require some work on the part of the householder, are giving way to meters that follow viewers remotely and record what they're watching (whenever and wherever) without the panelist having to do anything but pack the device along.

That's better, but not the Holy Grail, which might very well be coming. A single-source measuring system that compares consumers' purchases with what ads they've watched was tested in 2006. Project Apollo, developed by Nielsen parent VNU and Arbitron in collaboration with Procter & Gamble, PepsiCo, Unilever, SC Johnson, Pfizer, and Kraft, ran a pilot with 6,250 households from December 2005 through June 2006. Their data enabled the marketers to figure out if they were putting their money in the right place specifically and generally (the industry standard mix for marketing expenditure allocation is 28.5 percent for consumer promotion, 17.5 percent for advertising, and 54 percent on trade marketing and promotion).

Finally, to see why ratings are overrated, look at how all of this time is sold. During the same month of May when networks are throwing all kinds of ratings gimmicks at buyers, each of the broadcast and television networks begins what is called "the Upfronts." In other words, television sales executives want to sell all of their time *upfront* and in advance. And they want to do it during May when their shows are getting the highest ratings.

So, months before most marketers have a grasp of their upcoming budgeting and planning, in cold-pizza-fueled late-night gun-to-the-head negotiations cemented around fears of double-digit price increases in the scatter market (leftover market), advertisers stampede to spend half to two-thirds of their ad budgets based on little more than the snake-oil showmanship of the networks. But what brilliant snake oil it is, complete with glitzy stage shows and performances.

With these upfronts, the networks have been able to turn what are essentially commodities like orange juice or pork bellies into *pièces de resistance*—without anyone knowing for sure what programs will actually be on the air in the fall. Unlike Seventh Avenue fall runway shows where buyers place orders for specific garments, network schedules are a continuing work in progress. What buyers see in these glitzy smoke-and-mirror samplers bears little relationship to what they'll get in the fall.

The frenzy and tumult of upfront defies reason. It's not just because the networks demand a fourth-to-first-quarter commitment—no company plans that way—or that the commitments are made before the real schedules are known—no company buys that way—or that no significant paper trail exists to trace the buying process—no company manages that way—but because advertisers do not know the market price of what they're buying. No company spends money that way.

Unlike a true "open" market where buyers know what things cost, in the TV upfront market, advertisers know only how much they're paying. And different advertisers pay different prices based on what they paid the year before, adjusted for market demand. The true *market price* of television is actually the average of advertiser-paid prices. But only the networks (and one or two of the larger media-buying agencies) know what that market price is. And they're not telling. They claim the information is confidential. (One agency even claimed that the pricing data for a client's television buys were its "intellectual property" and not for release.) "Would you want us to give your data to a competitor?" they ask.

The answer, of course, is that concealed pricing is central to the current good-old-boy upfront process that has netted the broadcast networks more than nine billion dollars in each recent upfront season—and the cable networks more than six billion. (Such irrational success has spawned clones. By late 2005, AOL had sold out advertising spots for its In2TV classic TV programming through 2006. Yahoo! and MSN sold out their entertainment, financial services, and travel sections for the year by February, and more than 75 percent of cinema advertising inventory goes between October and December.)

However, there is hope, and it can be found in two news headlines from late May 2006. *The Wall Street Journal* reported on May 15, 2006:

J&J TO SKIP NETWORK TV'S "UPFRONT" MARKET

The annual network "upfront" ad-selling season officially kicks off today, but one of the country's biggest advertisers won't be buying—at least not now.

The second headline was reported by *MediaDailyNews* on May 12, 2006:

EBAY WINS BID TO TEST ONLINE MEDIA BUYING SYSTEM

Days after an ad industry task force unveiled plans to test an electronic trading system for buying and selling media, online auction giant eBay has won the bid.

Now, when the slick and well-dressed network television sales executives think of eBay PowerSellers, they mostly think of overweight, tacky, and somewhat crazed middle-aged Red State women selling Beanie Babies. At the very least, they think of the 10,000 zealots who travel each year to Las Vegas to attend eBay Live! These people cram into a giant arena and cheer for the always professional but never glitzy Meg Whitman.

Well, we have only one thing to say to network television sales executives: Welcome to eBay Live!

Really, what is difference between an eBay seller auctioning recycled golf balls and ABC auctioning air time on *Grey's Anatomy*?

An open market would give buyers better information, and probably result in lower television costs, just as open markets have done everywhere else. More than half of advertisers claim to be so dismayed with the up-front process that they want the system dramatically overhauled.

Changes will come, but slowly unless a lot more big buyers like Johnson & Johnson bail on the upfront scrum. It needs an army of buyers saying *no!*

Ratings are overrated because the entire system for buying advertising on television is changing. Five years from now, the upfronts will be auctions. They'll still be glitzy and feature William Shatner singing, but following the show, the electronic auction will begin and everyone will get something better. Advertisers will get better prices and the hottest shows will get the best bids.

Meanwhile, the army of advertisers is swatting at another distraction. In the near future, TV won't be bought and sold on eyeballs, but on engagement. In pioneer projects in 2005, Court TV and The Weather Channel guaranteed they'd reach a set number of viewers *and* achieve some level of viewer engagement. In the early days of formulating the rules of engagement, every buyer and network had a different and proprietary way to calculate viewer engagement. Several ad institutions like the Advertising Research Foundation, the American Association of Advertising Agencies, and the Association of National Advertisers aim to come up with a single measurement.

Admittedly Carat has a research tool, Foretel, to measure viewer involvement, but engagement in a TV show might have no bearing on whether the viewer decides to buy an advertised product. That has prompted some companies such as IAG Research to try to measure the effectiveness of advertising in other ways, like viewer attentiveness and recall. The networks are also weighing in. ABC's M14 lets buyers zoom in on rating points that represent buyers more likely to buy specific products. CBS is studying how product placement in a show increases the effectiveness of the ad in it and NBC is focusing on how engaged viewers are during commercials.

While that research unfolds, advertisers are angling for beachfront property in commercial pods. Studies have shown that viewers recall the first and last commercials in a break better than those mashed in the middle. But several networks try to keep the "A" positions for their own promos, which they conveniently don't count as ads (viewers do, however). Advertisers also want the commercial pods to be shorter. Now the commercial breaks are so long that viewers are conditioned to leave the room when they come on. (The usual 30-minute show has eight minutes of ads.)

They're also looking to squeeze any advantage from a system in flux. Even the concept of the September-though-May TV season (which developed to coincide with new-car launches and the school year) is changing. New programs now birth year-round. And summer, when viewership traditionally dips 10 to 20 percent, is now less about reruns and more about experimentation as broadcasters have recognized they cannot allow cable companies to siphon away any more viewers.

Changes *will* roil the sweeps world, too. With far fewer precious shows that command audiences to assemble simultaneously around the electronic hearth (like the *Super Bowl*) and fewer marketers that need Friday exposure to generate Saturday sales (like movies), there will be less upfront demand. Indeed, demand will have a very long tail.

And while sweeps has been likened to a QWERTY keyboard—a holdover from another era—with detailed demographics available to advertisers the next day, there'll be no need for extravaganzas and breathless special reports that have tarted up those time periods. Instead, the retail calendar will assure that certain times of the year, such as pre-Christmas, have lots of must-see programming.

So, for you couch potatoes, enjoy the gimmicks and naked co-anchors now, because ratings are overrated and times are a-changing.

5

WHY NEWSPAPERS HATE CRAIG AND HIS INFAMOUS "LIST"

On January 4, 2006, we, along with millions of others, awoke to exultant news. MIRACLE IN MINE: TWELVE FOUND ALIVE 41 HOURS AFTER BLAST, beamed the *Atlanta Journal Constitution*. SUDDENLY, THERE IS JOY: 12 MINERS FOUND ALIVE, blared the *Los Angeles Times*. RESCUED! 12 MINERS ALIVE AFTER TWO DAYS UNDERGROUND, brayed the *New York Daily News*. And there it was, on page one of *The New York Times*: 12 MINERS FOUND ALIVE 41 HOURS AFTER EXPLOSION.

We'd all gone to sleep the night before fearful about the fate of the trapped Sago, West Virginia, coal workers and awoke fearful about the fate of newspapers. In an era of instant messaging, they look like lumbering dinosaurs with a lot more to worry about than Craig's List. For on the radio, TV, online—everywhere—was the *real* news that morning, that except for one lucky survivor, all the miners had perished.

During the 2005 terrorist attacks on London's tube, trapped passengers stealthily snapped photos with their mobile phones and wirelessly uploaded them to Yahoo!'s photo-sharing site Flickr. Within minutes they were posted on Yahoo!'s news sites. Hot off the press just isn't fast enough anymore.

So if it's not news that newspapers can offer, what exactly is it? It's not advertising or a sense of community either, as modern-day flower-child Craig Newmark and his infamous list have demonstrated.

Craig Newmark, who by all accounts including his own is a nebbish geek, never expected that his "list" would be anything more than a simple, benign, hopefully beneficial service for folks who needed a place to live or had something to sell. But what he unleashed in 1995 in San Francisco "just trying to give people a break" has galvanized newspapers into defense mode.

Crowned the Exploder of Journalism, Craig Newmark is wreaking havoc with the advertising side of big-city newspapers as well. His list, Craigslist.org, where young urban people come to find an apartment or roommate, a lost pet or lover, a job or job-sharer, or each other has assaulted what may be the most profitable part of newspaper advertising. In 2005, newspaper classifieds brought in $17 billion. Craigslist's free or really cheap postings—in open-source lingo, its *commons*—get more than three billion page-views a month from more than 10 million actual users. That's enough to make it the seventh most popular destination in cyberspace. In New York City alone Craigslist offers more than half a million available apartments every month.

Inspired by San Francisco's spirit of hi-tech experimentation and extreme volunteerism, Newmark embraced the concept of open-sourcing and, in 1995, began sending notices of techie get-togethers, lectures, and other juicy events to a dozen friends. The "friends" multiplied and so did the offerings. They grew to include jobs, domiciles, and other opportunities. Within a few months, there were more recipients on his list than the 240 e-mail ceiling for CCs. Newmark invested in a listserv, and named his site.

Once the list had attracted more than a million page-views a month, Microsoft asked to advertise on it. Newmark said no. But by 1999, he'd quit his day job to work full time building a community—and the trust that would sustain it. He turned his back on accepting display ads and on going public, essentially spurning enormous wealth. His community recognized this and urged him to charge modestly for listings to finance the operation. Now, posting a help-wanted or studio-to-rent ad costs $75 in San Francisco and $25 in New York, Los Angeles, and D.C. The dollars added up-to more than $20 million in 2006. That prompted the *San Francisco Weekly* to dub the site "Craig$list" and Microsoft, Google, and eBay to get busy developing clone services.

Newmark, who professes a desire not to hurt anyone, also threatens the newspapers' very journalistic raison d'être by advocating "citizen journalism," and opinion over objectivity. ("When a politician lies and you know it, say something about it," he beseeches.) The role of a newspaper should not be merely delivering information but connecting people and activating conversations. That he's demonstrated he has done. During the 2005 New York transit strike, the ride-share space of area newspapers was all but bare while Craigslist brimmed with some 800 offers.

Meanwhile, "citizen journalism" is exploding on its own. Perhaps its most successful example to date is *Ohmy News*, an online newspaper started in February 2000 as a reaction to the "closed and elitist journalistic culture" in South Korea. It gets 700,000 visitors and two million page-views a day—more than many large newspapers. But instead of a newsroom, reporters are everyday "netizens" compensated by a "tip-jar." Readers are invited to donate (via their mobile phone or credit card) for features they find especially worthy. (One article amassed $30,000 in five days.)

Craigslist, citizen journalism, the time lag between when news happens and when newspapers get it before their readers—these are some of the reasons that the circulations of most big city dailies have been drooping for the past four decades, especially among younger readers whom advertisers covet. The average weekday circulation for 18 of the country's top 20 newspapers dropped 2.6 percent from March to September 2005, and the circulation fall-off for Sunday was even steeper: 3 percent for the top 20 newspapers combined. (*The New York Times*, *USA Today* and *The Wall Street Journal* have largely held steady.)

Free newspapers are also to blame. Ride the London underground, Seoul metro, or New York's Lexington Avenue local during rush hour and you'll see commuters immersed in their giveaway tabloids. We've counted more than 100 new free big-city dailies in the last decade in more than two-dozen countries across Europe, South America, and Asia, and in Canada, Australia, and the United States. Here some of the freebies, like

Belo's Quick in Dallas or the *Washington Post's Express*, are miniversions of the paid paper created to keep encroachers out. That's in addition to the plethora of free dailies published for decades in small communities like Colorado ski towns. Swedish-based Metro International alone distributes more than 18.5 million each day in 21 countries, 17 languages, and 83 major cities.

Some of these freebies are handed out at bus and train stations; others are tossed on stoops and driveways. On its first day in 2006, *The Baltimore Examiner* claimed a larger circulation than its 169-year-old rival, *The Baltimore Sun* (260,000 vs. 247,193 copies) by virtue of its being dropped, unsolicited, onto doorsteps in only the area's upscale communities. The *Sun*, which lost 20,000 readers or almost 8 percent of its total circulation in 2005, has a newsroom of 340, more than a dozen Pulitzers, and an ad page that goes for around $17,000. The *Examiner's* staff of 20 or so turn out articles of 300 words or less and advertisers can run a full page for only $2,900.

Unlike traditional newspapers, these free dailies are magnets for younger readers. Metro claims that 74 percent of its readers are under age 49. They're attracted by the "news-lite" style of these fast reads: the quick-take news update as well as a dollop of celebrity, sports, entertainment, and services (weather, movie reviews and times, crosswords, comics, horoscopes). They know to leave the analysis and investigative reporting to others: A recent survey funded by Bayer found that 94 percent of people would rather hear good news than bad and more than three out of four believe traditional media doesn't cover the good news enough.

"We're not here to mobilize readers or change things," Metro CEO Pelle Tornberg has said. Nor, he admits, does he need to put bikini girls or crime shockers on the front page to sell papers. Instead, what he aims to do is to provide readers with a heavy dose of local coverage for a 20-minute commute at a price they find irresistible. Publishers who hope these morsels will whet their appetites enough to pay for more substantial fare are deluded. Research shows that half of the readers of these free papers don't pay to read another. Indeed, even as subscription prices are rising to offset rising production costs, the perceived value of traditional newspapers is eroding as people can, and do, get their news anywhere.

A disclaimer here: We are both newspaper junkies for whom the prospect of lying in, with the sections splayed about us, is sublime. But that's because we've grown up with the newspaper habit and the excitement of learning about something we didn't know. Our children have not.

Another reason for the circulation drop is the effectiveness of the do-not-call registry. As recently as 2000, telemarketing accounted for nearly 58 percent of all new newspaper subscribers, according to the Newspaper Association of America (NAA). That figure has since slimmed significantly.

The circulation attrition has so disconcerted newspapers—their readership numbers, after all, are what advertisers are buying—that some have taken draconian measures around it. Some, like the *San Francisco Chronicle* and *Des Moines Register*, did away with promotions and giveaways to deliberately slash their circulations and thereby trim their costs and improve their demographics. Others turned to the dark side. For weeks in 2004, *Newsday* hawkers on Long Island sold mass copies to "fake" motorists who were, in fact, the agents' own carriers, to fraudulently boost the daily's circulation. They also listed partial-week subscribers as seven-day recipients even when they didn't want the papers and regularly carried nonpaying customers on their delivery routes.

The ploy touched off federal investigations, forced *Newsday*'s parent, the Tribune Co., to pay aggrieved advertisers $95 million, and resulted in the dismissal of some offenders. It also led to the discovery that fudged collection reports and "carrying the load" were routine at other papers. *The Dallas Morning News* and *Chicago Sun-Times* were caught overstating their numbers. And in March 2006, in a circulation-pumping scheme, tens of thousands of *New York Posts* were dumped at recycling centers just hours after they were printed and on the eve of the final reporting day of the Audit Bureau of Circulations' reporting period.

The Audit Bureau of Circulations (ABC) is the czar of the newspaper industry, its three little letters omnipresent on any chart about print media. The Chicago-based group creates the rules by which magazines and newspapers play, and enforces them. You may have felt the ramifications. Take that *USA Today* sitting outside your hotel room door. Because of the ABC's adjudication, if you opt not to get the paper you're entitled to a $1 reduction in your room rate. There's no mass exit from, nor abandonment of, the nation's almost 1,500 daily newspapers the way there is of camera film, say. Newspapers still have a huge reach—their daily circulations hover around 55 million (with audiences that are better educated and wealthier than the norm), not counting the millions of online readers. Indeed, even with circulation declining, newspapers are still cash cows with profit margins that dwarf those of the average company. Goldman Sachs figures the profit margin for America's dozen biggest newspapers in a recent year was more than double that of the average Fortune 500 company. The McClatchy Group, for example, had 30.3 percent margins in 2005, considerably more than the 16 percent for ExxonMobil or the 4 percent of the typical supermarket.

To judge from the spin that the Newspaper Association of America puts on the circulation slump, you'd think it's negligible. They argue that readership is at an all-time high of 85 million if you factor in those visiting newspaper web sites (and they're developing measurement techniques that count newspapers' total reach and audience). And if you don't buy that, they claim the readership decline has abated since 1990, and at any rate, it's much less than what television network news has experienced of late. Furthermore, much of the shrinkage, the NAA maintains, was the result of the disappearance of evening papers.

While revenue from print ads remains robust—how does more than $47 billion in 2005 sound?—the patient is sneezing. One major U.S. retailer decided not to buy ads in local newspapers after a test in two states showed the retailer it wasn't worth it. Sales of its advertised loss-leader items soared, but with ultrathin margins, the chain said it couldn't offset the cost of the ads. What's more, the giant retailer feels it doesn't need to advertise in newspapers because customer traffic in its stores is so strong without it. Did we mention that newspapers, in a sort of affirmative action for local advertisers, charge all national advertisers a higher rate than they do local businesses?

While the discriminatory pricing may dampen Unilever's and Colgate's enthusiasm for newspapers, it's not cementing the loyalty of those

benefiting from the two-tier pricing. Research from the automotive industry delivers an even chillier message. New-car buyers are clicking their
way to auto dealerships' web sites—and moving away from newspaper
ads. Friedman-Swift Associates, a Cincinnati-based automotive marketing
research firm, found that in 2005, 30 percent of new-car buyers overall
and 36 percent of import purchasers visited dealer sites, compared with
35 percent who looked at dealers' much more costly ads in local newspapers. But in 2001, just 17 percent of prospective car buyers had visited a
dealer web site. Judy George, president of Friedman-Swift, predicted that
this behavior will steer dealerships' ad dollars away from newspapers.

Rather than cry uncle, the newspaper establishment is ripping up the
playbook and figuring out best practices. The American Press Institute-
sponsored Newspaper Next project has parceled out different problems
for a half-dozen newspapers to tackle. The *Hackensack, New Jersey Record,*
for example, is testing different ways to deliver more community-engage-
ment offerings online. *The Oregonian* in Portland is tinkering with what
works best to increase readership in a fast-growing suburb. Media General in Richmond, Virginia, is trying to identify what unique insights into
area problems its ad programs can solve.

Several papers have gone at it alone. *The Washington Post* shouldered
into radio. *Washington Post Radio AM-FM's* news updates rely heavily on interviews with *Post* reporters, making WTOP both a news source and a
continuous promotional vehicle for the paper.

For years, newspapers have wrapped full-page ads around their real
front page, but recently *The New York Daily News* ran real full-page ads for
Mazda and Toyota as the real front page, turning what had been a paper's
most valuable and heretofore sacred real estate into a revenue producer.
*The Wall Street Journal, Los Angeles Times, USA Today, New York Times, Boston
Globe,* and *Chicago Tribune* now allow ads on the front of some news sections—even the front page itself. That breaks a 50-year tradition in U.S.
newspapers, although ads on front pages and section fronts are common
in European, South American, and Asian newspapers.

Stock tables and TV magazines have been excised at many newspapers to cut production costs. Newspapers have gotten more concise,
more local, and more community specific. Some have launched Spanish

or Chinese editions with coverage on the native lands of the immigrant communities. They've also gone more interactive, adding feedback and conversation panes at the bottom of online articles and sponsoring blogs. The *Greensboro News & Record* even uses a steady stream of reader-written articles. The *Bluffton Today* paper from South Carolina offers RSS (Really Simple Syndication) feeds, podcasts, blogs, and a very successful "We Spotted/You Spotted" photo gallery that generates high engagement. And they've taken to buffing their web sites to a shine. Several of them have added news aggregation services online, offering stuff from elsewhere with links to the sites where they originated. *The Washington Post* web site already pulls in $2 billion a year.

Still, that's peanuts compared to the real bread-and-butter its paper form generates. Advertising revenue from newspapers dwarfs what they make from their web sites. (According to the Newspaper Association of America, just 5.5 percent of the newspaper industry's revenues come from their online divisions.) Even as their online dollars grow, no one thinks they'll come close to replacing what they've lost—and will continue to lose—from print. Analyst Lauren Rich Fine estimates that for every ad dollar a newspaper gets for a print reader, it receives only 20 to 30 cents for its online equivalent. As for circulation revenue, subscriptions and newsstand sales don't even begin to cover the cost of producing the papers.

Some $1.6 billion of newspaper ad revenue comes via Downers Grove, Illinois-based NSA (Newspaper Services of America), the 800-pound gorilla of the industry on the speed-dial of virtually every newspaper ad sales director. NSA buys and manages more newspaper insertions than any other company in America.

Philip Meyer, in his 2004 book, *The Vanishing Newspaper*, says the last reader will recycle the last newspaper in April 2040—eight years short of the printing press's 600th anniversary. We don't share Meyer's fatalistic prediction, but we strongly believe that newspapers will look a lot different tomorrow than they do today.

Like Craig Newmark, we suspect that many will be delivered electronically, perhaps via scrollable displays of cell phones with news tailored to each individual. Like Metro's Pelle Tornberg, we imagine they'll be more exclusive, with smaller circulations and bigger price tags, and perhaps only a weekend luxury. Like Philip K. Dick, who wrote the short story upon which the sci-fi *Minority Report* movie was based, we envision them as fully interactive, perhaps updating right before our eyes. Based on their deep knowledge of their community, we expect they'll go ultralocal. What we don't expect is for the words *news* and *paper* to exclusively coexist.

6

WHY OUTDOOR COMPANIES
PRAY FOR TRAFFIC JAMS

I n the Steven Spielberg film, *Minority Report*, cars run on magnets, virtual-reality stations abound, would-be murderers are arrested before they kill, and cops use "sick sticks" to bring them down. Did you also pay attention to the "smart sticks" in the movie—poster ads that recognized passersby and addressed them by name? That Big Brother vision may not be so far off now that digital is replacing glue and paper, and "interactive" is edging aside static billboards.

Outdoor advertising dates back to Jurassic times when some primordial dude drew pictures of wooly mammoths on the side of caves. It's obvious, thousands of years hence, that he wanted others to see his work. (It's not obvious whether some marketing-minded man arranged a lucrative sponsorship for his tribe or family unit from some loin-cloth manufacturer.)

A picture on a stick feels very smart in an age when consumers turn off ads. Now that the oversized, pretty "picture" is increasingly less something you just look at, and more something you can interact with, this in-your-face, TiVo-proof proposition packs even more punch, especially when you take into account traffic on the roads. Is there congestion on Route 80, or a backup on I-95? Clear Channel CEO Mark Mays can only smile. "People listen to more radio, and they have more time to look at billboards." Motorists, by definition, are a captive audience. Outdoor is not an on-demand medium. You can't choose to see it: You *have* to see it.

What they're seeing are more electronic billboards that change static messages dozens of times a day—up to once every eight seconds. That means that if you are gridlock bound, you're a marketer's mark. Clear Channel Outdoor has seven of these giant light-emitting-diode displays in Cleveland: That steaming Dunkin' Donuts coffee that commuters saw in the morning very likely could be a frothy Michelob on their ride home. Dillard's could decide impromptu to hold a clearance sale and promote whatever inventory it wants to unload.

These billboards, actually screens with a slideshow of ads like you see at movie theaters, dot roads in Pittsburgh, across Montana, and on many other byways. (These have no dancing or flashing images as in Las Vegas or the no-holds-barred street theater of Times Square in accordance with zoning board restrictions.) There were perhaps 100 LED billboards across America in 2005—out of more than 450,000 along the federal highway system. The Outdoor Advertising Association of America said they more than doubled in 2006 and will ultimately replace the vinyl boards, which themselves replaced those that were painted and wallpapered on.

These new smarter billboards are no larger than traditional billboards, and most drivers aren't even aware that they're different. But marketers surely are. And it's not just because they offer flexibility (before, you were stuck with the billboard or bus shelter for 30 days); it's because this ancient advertising medium is now being sold as time instead of space.

Instead of buying a monthly feature, they're purchasing a share of a continuously rotating loop of ads whose messages can change with the push of a button at some remote location, for a day-part. Ruth Chris Steak House came in for the 4-to-7-P.M. shift and Captivate Network sells ads on 6,500 flat-panel TVs in elevators where prime time is the middle of the workday. Captive can target specific buildings and change the message by either day-part or day of the week. On day one, an ad could talk about Volvo's safety; on day two, about its quality; and on day three, concentrate on its performance, and so on.

This is not some futuristic fantasy. It's here. NBC has already run "tune-in-tonight" promos for the premiere of Medium on motion-video plasma screens in Loew's Cineplex lobbies. AdSpace Media Networks has been installing those screens in shopping malls since 2003. The Minnesota Lottery continually updated its growing jackpot on LED screens that NextMedia Group has installed in the lounge areas of public bathrooms.

In the days when the Big Three TV networks dominated the media landscape, billboards were underused. Occasionally a great campaign found its way outdoors, like Burma Shave's, which ran from 1925 to 1963. Its messages were parsed across several signs, hooking the reader with the promise of an ultimate payoff or punchline. Here's one:

Shaving brushes
You'll soon see 'em
On a shelf
In some museum
Burma-Shave

The NCAA recently mimicked this approach, presenting a basketball player aiming a shot on one billboard; on the next one, 90 yards away, is the basket. Critics have long complained that these boards despoiled the roadside. Ogden Nash riposted: "I think that I shall never see a billboard lovely as a tree. Perhaps unless the billboards fall, I'll never see a tree at all." Under Lady Bird Johnson's initiative, Congress passed the Highway Beautification Act in 1965.

Back then, *outdoor* meant roadside billboards. Today, it could mean any of more than 200 formats, from ads on buses and their shelters to plaques atop and in taxis and on trains and signboard trucks, to coasters in bars, to shopping carts in supermarkets and kiosks in malls, airports, and sports stadiums, to wallscapes on buildings and "street furniture" like benches and even trash cans, à la ReceptaSigns in New York City. A Chicago museum attached ads to manhole covers to promote an exhibit that featured a German submarine. NYC sold ad rights on its newsstands and public toilets. Denver's Parking Stripe Advertising sold vinyl ads that cover the white stripes marking spaces in parking lots to Dell,

Halliburton, Qwest Communications, Ford, Home Depot, and PepsiCo on a CPS (cost-per-stripe) basis. Indeed, when it comes to outdoor, the world is a canvas.

In 1979, 39 percent of outdoor "faces" were covered with ads for cigarettes and another 19 percent promoted alcoholic beverages. In 1998, tobacco was still high on outdoor (accounting for 5% of total spending, down from its peak but still the top category), but a voluntary ban begun in April 1999 changed all that. Now, at least 7 out of 10 outdoor ads promote local businesses—it's an even higher percent in non-urban areas. Roadside restaurants and motels depend on these signs along interstates to spur "next exit" and "clean restrooms" action.

Many national advertisers have also begun to capitalize on the medium's capabilities. Mini Cooper's quirky "Let's Motor" boards may have spurred a creative resurgence here. Starbucks played off people's propensity to leave lattes on the roofs of cars by "forgetting" magnetic red coffee cups on a fleet of cabs. Yahoo! Personals hosted live dates on a Sunset Boulevard billboard. HBO wrapped the interior of New York's Shuttle train in *Deadwood*-era décor to pitch its drama. McDonald's milkshakes visually exude thickness. A Coca-Cola billboard waves back when passersby salute it. *Star Wars* posters integrating sound and motion brought Darth Vader to life before unsuspecting bus travelers in London.

To introduce its Zephyr, Lincoln-Mercury ran an in-tunnel motion picture campaign in the New York subway system. To introduce its 2006 Civic, Honda affixed 15-second motion pictures to existing scaffolding. Hawkers wearing flat-screen LCD TV vests advertising HSBC parade around Grand Central Terminal and Penn Station. And on a 23-story tower sign in Times Square, Nike invited passersby to customize shoes that they could later buy online. At that same crossroads of the world, Mountain Dew turned a billboard into an event by inviting passersby to have their picture taken as if they were part of the ad.

Technological boons like this are one reason the oldest mass medium is growing faster than all others, save for online and product placements. In 2004, outdoor made up only 2.3 percent of ad dollars spent in the United States; by 2005 it was 5.5 percent, and in 2006, more than $6 billion. By 2008, it's on target to snag $7.1 billion. The fact that, as a rule, comparable audiences cost advertisers around one-fifth of what they'd spend on prime-time TV is another reason for the boom. And our society has become increasingly mobile: Despite all the talk of cocooning and the construction of McMansions, we're spending more time away from home than in it.

Then too, services like Arbitron and Nielsen and the Traffic Audit Bureau have begun to furnish audience insights. Nielsen Outdoor, for example, equipped consumers with cell-phone-sized GPS devices called Npods when they walk or drive. The travel-log data that these devices generate is linked to traffic estimates to determine the number of passersby likely to see the ads. These GPS-based meters are also able to determine where a person is, what direction she's coming from, and how fast she's moving when she spies the billboard.

Of course, the medium has demonstrated effectiveness. Several years ago, a billboard company plastered a big picture of "Sharlene Wells, Miss America" all over town to cover up all the unsold boards *and* show how well its boards worked. The posters hung for a month. In surveys before (i.e., "unaided" recall), only 1.5 percent of people could answer, "Who is Miss America?" After the billboard barrage, 12 percent could identify the reigning beauty queen.

Now that the medium is increasingly interactively engaging consumers on the go, you don't need a survey to show its effectiveness. What began as a simple 2-D sign can now talk to you (via short-wave radio links), download data into your Palm Pilot (through a patented Street Beam device), connect you to the Web (via taxi tops), and change messages as you stroll past (through motion detection). Initially posters began including URLs. Then they moved on to simple push-button technology so they could play music or squirt perfume, and then to digital touch-screens. Now, Bluetooth wireless technology—based on a radio frequency transceiver—lets marketers open a dialogue with consumers via their cell phone, BlackBerry, or other mobile device. Bluetooth can send text, video, animated graphics, flash graphics, and readable bar codes. Passengers at Heathrow Airport can switch it on and opt to receive video trailers from Volvo. While only about 14 percent of U.S. phones are currently Bluetooth-enabled, by 2007, almost one in three will be. So marketers like Volvo have to hatch some incentives to make consumers at train stations, escalators, shopping malls, festivals, or football stadiums during downtime want to turn on their cell phone's Bluetooth capabilities and download its *Life On Board* documentary.

Bluetooth and RFDI technology are transitional tools: In the not-too-distant future, billboards will talk directly to your cell phone, PDA, or iPod. And in that era, optical recognition technology will let advertisers change their messages depending on the gender or age of the person approaching or his or her distance from the screen. Already Alaris Media Networks has a monitoring system inside LED billboards in California that tracks what radio station is on in your car and adjusts its ad message to jell with what it has learned. Drivers have no idea that Mobiltrak is tracking them. Pretty soon, Alaris says its board will be able to relay information to others further down the road to display the most appropriate ads to approaching traffic.

A few years ago, an anonymous spiritualist who knew that billboards are the only medium out there you can't avoid, tried to motivate others to think about divinity. He or she created "God Speaks" billboards with witty statements "signed" by God, like "Don't make me come down there," and "We need to talk." The messenger knew what outdoor companies do—that billboards work best in traffic. "Keep using my name in vain, and I'll make rush hour longer," one billboard promised.

7

WHY THE SUPER BOWL
IS STILL SUPER

T he biggest story of 2004 wasn't the Madrid bombings, the Abu
Ghraib prison scandal, the weather disasters in Asia, or the in-
surgency in Iraq. It was "Nipplegate" that generated the most
media coverage and consumer outrage. Janet Jackson's
"wardrobe malfunction," which then-FCC-Chairman Michael Powell
called a "classless, crass, and deplorable stunt," generated the biggest
spike in viewer reaction that TiVo had ever measured. For the first time in
NFL history, the halftime had stolen the show.

It also changed it for future marketers and programming. Safety
became the byword in the form of aging rock stars and noncontrover-
sial ads.

Roughly 90 million Americans and another 50 million from other
countries watched the New England Patriots battle the Carolina Panthers
in what has become known as the Super Bowl of Advertising. The crown-
ing glory of American football, it is the most anticipated, most watched,
most influential, most costly, and most anachronistic institution on television. Oddly, this relic of old ways and days still thrives in this age of virtually limitless viewing options, unprecedented viewer control over when
to watch, and unmatched disdain for traditional advertising.

When it began in 1967, the Super Bowl was hardly an advertising end-zone. There were 40,000 empty seats at the Los Angeles Coliseum (although the top admission price was only $12) and advertisers had to be sweet-talked into playing here. Today, of course, almost half the homes in America hunker down to watch, and it's been that way for a while. Eight of the 11 most-watched programs in U.S. TV history were Super Bowls. While the action on the field is rarely super, the ads often are and have been ever since McIntosh launched its Apple computer with the now-infamous "Why 1984 Won't Be Like 1984" spot during the scrimmage. The expectation of great advertising is why one in four viewers claims to tune in.

Marketing is so much a part of the action that companies line up to buy *portions* of the show: the Charles Schwab Corp. pre-kickoff, for example, in 2000; the E-Trade halftime show; the Pontiac post-game cooldown. The stadiums where the games are played are often named after a sponsor. In fact, it's not the players, fans, or broadcasters who have the best time here: It's the sponsors and their agents. Media buyers are courted like royalty. One year at an ESPN party, my orthopedic-surgeon brother huddled with Joe Theisman discussing his knee injury while Boomer Esiason sat next to me and the Dallas Cowboys cheerleaders twirled around us.

For most people, Super Bowl Sunday is the one day that advertising becomes a friend and not a party crasher. Actually, the cease-fire against advertising begins weeks before the game and continues for a few days afterward, as people enjoy Super Bowl sales, specials, recipes, postmortems, get-togethers (more at-home parties even than on New Year's Eve), food (Thanksgiving is the only day on which more is eaten), and legends (water-system shutdowns from simultaneous toilet flushing at halftime). Hyped by hoopla, people talk about these ads before they air as well as afterward. Multivision Inc. says the number of media pieces about Super Bowl ads tripled from 2003 to 2005.

That makes the investment (an MSRP of around $2.4 million for 30 seconds) easier to swallow. No one actually pays the asking price, however. A $2.2 million asking price will actually sell for around $1.9 million. Ads in the first half generally cost more and every sharp advertiser insists on being there—and takes it out on the agency if the network shuffles it into a later showing. The mediaocracy know that those in the fourth quarter either have no clout or got a giant discount. Where an ad is positioned in a pod also influences the cost, with the first spot in a commercial break selling for more than one buried in the middle of the pack.

The price is getting harder to justify. In 2006, marketers did it by sending viewers to their web sites to engage them further. After the game, budweiser.com traffic grew 594 percent, with heady spikes at cadillac.com, ameriquestmortage.com, and subway.com.

But the Super Bowl is not an investment made for purely rational or objective reasons. From a purely mathematical perspective, the divisional playoffs are a far better value. Figure a 40 rating for $2 million for 30 seconds compared to a 20 rating for $600,000 to $700,000.

Rather, advertisers come here to reach a huge, unduplicated swath of America at once (40% of the audience is female and three out of four are not traditional football fans) for approximately $9 per thousand viewers, and get a bevy of intangibles to boot. On the day after the game, people remember the commercials more than twice as well as they recall the average prime-time spot, and they like them better, too. But perhaps most critical, the Super Bowl is watched live as it's played, ads intact, rather than taped to be played back on a DVR where the ads are usually skipped. That's the reasoning I gave the Alamo client when in 1994, while at the Hal Riney agency, I bought the only 90-second spot ever to run in the game for $2.7 million.

Still, there is the price for ads (*and* tickets), the commercial clutter, and the folly of the excess to consider. It's why some advertisers, like Frito-Lay, have done end-runs. (In 1992, it sponsored a special half-hour episode of *In Living Color* that began just as the Super Bowl's halftime did.) Others have advertised in less-costly blockbusters like the Academy Awards (aka the "Super Bowl for Women"), the World Series, the Olympics, and the emerging dynamo, the annual National Collegiate Athletic Association basketball tournament. In 2006, advertisers bet $500 million on the 63 games of March Madness—up from $311 million in 2000.

But not all blockbusters have fared as well as the Super Bowl. NBC paid $614 million for rights to broadcast the Winter Olympics in 2006, expecting to generate $900 million in ad revenue. But even before the opening ceremonies concluded, we knew who lost. Rival networks, which in the past had rolled over and played dead in the face of this Olympian force, now attacked. Like a tsunami gushing over the landscape, they flooded prime time with "appointment TV," including new episodes of *Survivor, Dancing With the Stars, Desperate Housewives, Grey's Anatomy, Lost, 24, House,* and, as if to rub salt in, seven hours on five nights of *American Idol.* Four years earlier, CBS, sensing the foolishness of hurling anything against the Olympics, had delayed until the games were over to unveil a new *Survivor.*

The networks had studied the games more attentively than the bookies, and had determined that the Olympics were vulnerable. Few personalities other than skier Bode Miller had energized the public, the time difference from Turin meant that anyone could find out the results before the races were broadcast, and NBC, in the ratings cellar, could not promote the Olympics with the bravado, gusto, or impact that it did four years earlier when it was at the top of its game. Over its 17-day run, the Winter Games averaged 20 percent fewer viewers than did the previous overseas Winter Olympics in Nagano in 1998.

Despite its hoopla, the 2006 Academy Awards broadcast didn't deliver on its "must-see" promise either. Fewer than 39 million viewers—the event's second-smallest audience in nearly two decades and three million less than a year earlier—tuned in to see Hollywood take the field. Unlike in 1998, when more than 55 million watched *Titanic* sink the competition, most of the 2006 nominees were more niche than mainstream. Before the ceremony that seems to last longer than the Super Bowl, fewer people had seen *Brokeback Mountain, Capote, Good Night, and Good Luck, Munich,* and winner *Crash* collectively than had seen just the most recent *Star Wars* movie.

On the other hand, even when a team from nowhere makes it to the Big Game, the audience still shows up. And that's what makes the Super Bowl a super ad event.

Live sports and event programming will remain part of our culture and mountains on the media range, but the double-digit price increases of Super Bowls past are history. From here on, we expect there'll be ad time available in every game and smart advertisers will wait on the sidelines to jump in for discounted deals.

The focus, too, may change to reveal more about the behind-the-scenes life of the games or blockbuster events—green-room kind of fare. Take the Olympics, with 3,000 testosterone-charged athletes inside the Olympic village. Now that's a party we want to go to . . . or at least watch on TV.

PART TWO

A WHOLE NEW BALL GAME

8

WHY GOOGLE HAS UPSET
THE APPLE CART

I t wasn't supposed to be this way. When two Stanford software engineer grad students conceived the search engine "BackRub" (nick-
named because it checked back-links to estimate a web site's
importance), they reasoned that a search engine that analyzed relationships between web sites would get better results than what was out
there, which tabbed results to how often the search term appeared on a
page. At the time, Larry Page and Sergey Brin disdained advertising-
funded search engines as "inherently biased toward advertisers and away
from needs of consumers," and reluctantly included them in their business
plan as the safety net for their entrepreneurial scheme.

That safety net has turned into a veritable trampoline. In just eight
years, the world's largest Internet search company (named after a mis-
spelling of *googol*, which is 1 followed by 100 zeros) had a market capital-
ization of some $120 billion in June 2006 and was twice as big as
runner-up Yahoo! The name has entered several languages as a generic
verb for the act of searching. By creating an efficient, automated way to
sell ads that target consumers with what they most want to see, Google
came to dominate the $12 billion Internet ad market and become the
fourth-largest advertising vehicle out there. Its 2006 ad revenue of $9.5

billion put it behind Viacom, News Corp., and Walt Disney Co., but ahead of NBC Universal and Time Warner.

Fueled by fear that online searchers are merely one click away from defecting to competitors, and that 99 percent of its revenues are from advertising, this octopus is growing new media tentacles and wriggling into other facets of online life. Google has moved into e-mail and instant messaging, word processing and spreadsheets, and price comparison and payments. Its Google Maps trail only MapQuest in mapping-site traffic. Its Google News is the second-most-trafficked news aggregation site on the Internet.

Users of Google Co-op can sign up for free health bulletins from venerable organizations like the Mayo Clinic and Kaiser Permanente or city guide information for more than 300 cities, including London and New York. Its Desktop 4 comes with more than 100 gadgets that let users do things such as list friends' birthdays, show videos, and play music. Google Notebook lets people save a portion of a web site to a box that can be shared with others, and Google Trends lets users examine searches for market trends.

There's also Google Earth, Google Calendar, Google Finance, Google Blog Search, Google Site Targeting, Google Froggle (its shopping search engine), and Orkut (Google's social-networking site). (Google search is coming to mobile phones.) More recently the giant has been infiltrating the radio, publishing, and TV ad markets with its trump cards: heft and the ability to link ads to relevant content. Just as its plans to digitize out-of-print books triggered suits from book publishers, everywhere the behemoth turns, intimidated competitors, whose turf it has invaded, quake.

When Google surfaced, AltaVista was the dominant search engine. It required users to construct labyrinthic search statements, such as "Madonna and not singer" for articles about Mary Magdalene. Google simplified the query process and delivered better results by analyzing how often web sites are linked to other highly ranked sites.

In 2000, when Google began selling ads, they were 10 to 12-word snippets of text that might be the engineering equivalent of Madison Avenue. Although they were designed to keep pages uncluttered and loading quickly, these text ads were so basic and unimaginative that automakers shooed the Google team away: They wanted ads that showed the chrome. (Somewhat ironically, recent Pontiac ads urged consumers to "Google Pontiac" because General Motors liked the credibility, consumer empowerment, and cachet of associating with the search engine.)

The ads were linked to topics associated with the search keyword. Ads above search results migrated to the right side of the page. Fixed prices migrated to an auction-based system where advertisers paid only if their ad was clicked on. But instead of giving priority to advertisers that bid the most per click, Google gave its most coveted real estate to ads it knew would bring in the most money—a combination of price bid and clickthrough. Revenue rocketed (but that rocket may hit astral dust as other search engines have mimicked Google in incorporating a relevancy component into their paid search ad. Yahoo!'s, in particular, is a clone of Google's).

Some of its services have already fattened Google's till in inventive ways. In late 2005 through early 2006, Carat Australia used Google's Earth satellite photography application, which gives users a bird's-eye view of the world, for Adidas to promote its official ball for the World Cup games. Consumers answered quiz questions about global football stars while Google Earth hopped between relevant locations to give clues. Google Trends, which on many days performs more than a million analyses, is employed by advertisers launching marketing campaigns, getting instant feedback from huge online focus groups, and then adjusting their messages based on that information. By affording the ability to check the relative popularity of any search term and mark how it's brightened or faded, Google Trends would give its users a leg up if they were betting on Taylor Hicks as the most recent *American Idol*. (He was searched more often than runner-up Katharine McPhee, who beat out Elliot Yamin, who came in third in the show and in search volume.)

Google expects that 60 to 80 percent of its new services will fizzle, but not all of them are designed to generate revenue. Google Checkout (or "GBuy," its online payment-processing capability launched in June

2006) was conceived primarily as a free value-add to advertisers who buy keyword ads through its AdWords program. But it also gives Google the crucial information of how many clickthroughs lead to purchases. And that information empowers it to jettison cost-per-click and the problematic issue of click fraud, and adopt cost-per-action pricing. That means it can charge higher rates based on whether the sales are completed.

Some security-conscious consumers won't shop online at all or at sites they don't trust, and 60 percent of Internet shoppers bail at checkout, exasperated by a tedious checkout process. Having the reliable Google store customer credit cards and shipping information (and not share it with retailers) and track orders should relieve their anxiety and speed the transaction. Google-as-middleman holding their online wallets should also tighten the relationship with consumers.

This capability did, however, choke Google's relationship with one of its principal customers. Online auction site eBay, which has bought keywords for nearly every sort of merchandise it sells, banned its buyers and sellers from using what analysts had dubbed the "embryonic PayPal killer," under threat of having their listings canceled, forfeiting their fees, or even having their entire account suspended.

That relationship had been on the ropes since November 2005, when Google Base (GBase) debuted in the $100 billion classified ad arena. GBase lets Internet users post classified and help-wanted ads for free. With GBase, instead of people putting up web pages and waiting for Google to find and search, anyone can type information into Google's computers, telling Google what search queries should locate that content, in virtually no time. Hypothetically, someone could use GBase to find a job and rent an apartment, buy a car there, land a date, and figure out where to go on it. While newspapers regarded it as a frontal attack on their lucrative revenue stream, PayPal also felt the giant's breath closer than it wanted.

Microsoft also found itself in the path of the lumbering giant when Google released free spreadsheets and the Google Pack, a suite of software to equip new PCs with basics including a web browser and antivirus software. MSN picked up the gauntlet. It recreated its AdCenter to take on Google, targeting ads demographically via its huge base of Hotmail and MSN users, first in search and then in video games and on TV.

Alas, Google Video is already there with a "download-for-a-fee TV show" formula, giving Apple's iTunes a dose of heebie-jeebies. Promising to democratize video sales, Google Video allows anyone, from the leading TV network to a lad with a video camera, to sell their productions. Google takes a percent of the sale for handling the technical server grunt work. Although in its infancy it lacked ratings, parental controls, recommendations, categories, customer comments, or even uniform resolution and quality, Google's video emporium quickly became the third-most-used video-sharing stop on the Web, according to Nielsen.

It's hard to imagine that Google has no ulterior motives or further ambitions here and that it won't take its search-based strengths—measurement, metrics, and ease of creation—and apply them in the video space. Indeed, Google CEO Eric Schmidt has said that when he watches TV now "it seems that all sports fans are only interested in beer. We think there's a better way to target." Because it knows what you watch and where you live—and can learn even more from TV set-top boxes, Google can create algorithms to figure out the type of car you might buy and serve up tailored ads of vehicles in your so-called consideration set. And by helping surfers locate and organize all available online video, they'll be better equipped to watch what they want, when they want. Some analysts see in Google Video the handwriting on the wall for traditional TV time, and liken the networks to the prime-time equivalent of Kodak's dying 35mm film business.

Google has already surfaced on the radio dial, by buying dMarc Broadcasting and striking fear into the hearts of the two national radio rep firms, Katz Media and Interep. Together, they handled around a fifth of the country's annual radio ad revenue. Before the acquisition, dMarc was a major media-buying service, with over 500 stations in its network for which it automatically sold, scheduled, and delivered radio ads on unsold inventory at the click of a mouse, letting advertisers bypass traditional agencies and media buyers. It also provides advertisers with real-time reports on when and how often an ad has aired on a particular station, something that used to take months to receive.

Now it's meshing with Google's computer power to determine how many open radio spots are available the night before, and upload paying customers. This brings the stations and Google welcome cash, better measurability and accountability in radio advertising, and a platform for more sophisticated targeting. dMarc's ability to splice in ads and Google's knowledge of customer demographics could make radio the first of many media platforms in the digital network to receive tailored ads.

Google has also ventured outside the digital network to the publishing world, where it acts as something of an arbitrageur. Again, its focus is remnant space. Dispensing entirely with publishers' rate cards, Google buys unsold space in newspapers and magazines directly from them, then auctions it to top bidders, promising to work with successful bidders "to fill your ad space effectively." It makes money if advertisers offer more than Google paid.

Google also tested small search-type ads in the business and sports sections of the *Chicago Sun-Times* that direct readers to web sites.

But the two drivers of its ad bounty are AdWords and AdSense. The former cost-per-click service hit it big when it debuted in February 2002, as Google's third crack at an ad auction. Here advertisers choose and bid for keyword terms—"Indianapolis tailor" or "Seattle acupuncturist," for instance—that bring up their ads next to search results and as sponsored links. Unlike typical first-price auctions, where the highest sealed bid pays his or her bid (and can end up with winner's remorse), the second-price auction that AdWords adopted penalizes the highest bidder by only a penny.

Advertisers pay Google only when a web surfer clicks on an ad. This concept is enormously popular with my clients. In TV, we guess who watched an ad. With Google, we pay only for actions taken. No wonder Google's revenues have taken off like a rocket ship.

The golden goose of AdWords is Google Analytics, which enables marketers to measure the performance of their online ads by reporting on keyword performance and substituting accountability for guesswork. Google's Web analytics tools track page-views and user behavior, and measure site traffic by metrics including geography, time of day, and more. With this tool Discount Tire could tell immediately how visitors entered and exited the site, what they were doing once they clicked on a text ad, which pages worked best and which ones tripped them up, and where and why they gave up on making a purchase. Discount Tire was then able to fix what wasn't optimal and convert more tire-kickers into buyers.

Google upgrades AdWords every two weeks to bring in new clients or to give existing ones more options. For example, it devised a starter edition to get small advertisers to create an ad and begin running it on Google in less than five minutes. To jazz up local business ads, it provides maps directing customers to stores. Most retailers advertise only 5 percent of their stuff, Google members are fond of saying. Google can let them advertise all of it.

Google's AdSense program, introduced later in 2002, provides a way for unrelated web sites and blogs to make money by hosting Google-supplied ads it has determined are relevant to the content on their web pages. For every page it shows, more than 100 of its computers evaluate more than a million variables to choose what ads in its database to display—and they do it in milliseconds. When people click on the ads, Google pays the web site a fee. When Paramount Pictures wanted to promote its movie, *Hustle & Flow*, the studio chose 100 small sites fed by AdSense to provide relevant ads.

Occasionally, AdSense's ads are perhaps *overly* relevant. Spain El Pais Google ads ran alongside an article on immigrant trafficking, touting mortgages for immigrants and European boat rentals and services for canoeists. And some years back a Samsonite ad appeared next to a story about body parts being found in a suitcase.

While Google is the undisputed leader in search (factoring in its investment in AOL it has at least half the market here and all expectations are that it will remain king), and search is the most lucrative activity on the Net, Google would seem to be on Easy Street. Rather, it's paying a steep price for upsetting the apple cart. For one thing, people expect great things from it. Mediocre from Google elicits brickbats. People go to Google to find information fast. So it can't showcase its new products without jeopardizing that ease of entry and its popularity. And when things go awry, it's the leader who takes the heat.

That it did when online advertisers filed a class-action lawsuit against web search companies they claimed overcharged them for click fraud (i.e., for when their ads were clicked by cutthroat competitors and automated systems to drive up the advertiser's cost). In mid-2006, Google agreed to credit all advertisers in its network since 2002 with $90 million worth of free ads.

As the weighty gorilla with the power to disrupt businesses wherever it treads, Google is in everyone's viewfinder. A not-insignificant enemy, Microsoft, regards Google as a mortal threat and has vowed to surpass it by redefining search and online advertising. It is, for example, exploring how to let PC users click on a set of pruning shears and get transported to a web site that sells the garden tool, and toying with ways to deliver extensive demographic profiles to online advertisers.

Google co-founder Larry Page downplays the rivalry with Microsoft, and contends that while some businesses have been threatened by its new, better way of doing business, others have emerged *because* of Google. SEO (Search Engine Optimization) has come about because of the new opportunities it laid bare, and other cottage industries include helping small sellers place products on its GBase. Fledgling production companies and search keyword managers should spring up. Carat has added new staffers to analyze how much the keyword cost, how many times it was clicked on, and how much traffic it generates to really understand the lifetime value of search customers. The agency has also worked with AOL extensively to track how customers who enter AOL sites via keyword search ads cross-pollinate across different AOL properties and return over time.

Besides, Page has said, 98 percent of what will exist a decade down the road has yet to be done. Google won't get to do it by looking at what other companies are doing.

This seems correct on one account. Looking over its shoulder at other, perhaps smarter technologies like "implicit query" search, which anticipates and hones inquiries from key words, and "smart folders," which automatically accumulate material of interest to the user, these seem more frightening than the hooves of well-known and entrenched opponents who are attempting to catch up to them. After all, Google itself got into search late and managed to squash many established rivals.

9

WHY WIKIPEDIA TICKS OFF THE OTHER MEDIA

Mere minutes after word that Kenneth Lay had died suddenly at his Colorado home six weeks after being convicted of fraud, Wikipedia reported that the disgraced CEO of Enron was "an apparent suicide." Within a half hour the obit in the online encyclopedia was edited several times to explain his demise as either a "heart attack or suicide," "the guilt of ruining so many lives finaly [*sic*] led him to suicide," "a doctor" blaming the "stress" of his trial, or the report that Lay's pastor attributed it to a massive coronary. The heart attack detail, whether true or not, stuck here, as it did in traditional media.

Wikipedia may be the antithesis of traditional *anything*. At this writing the 17th-most-popular site on the Internet, it serves up more than five billion pages a month and generates more traffic daily than MSNBC.com and the online versions of the *New York Times* and *Wall Street Journal* combined. Some days it gets 14,000 hits each second. Fueled by its high placement in Google searches, its visitor count has been doubling every four months.

When Jimmy Wales launched Wikipedia in 2001, he aimed to "distribute a free encyclopedia to everyone on the planet in their own language." It's well on its way toward that end, with editions in more than

200 languages already, and hundreds of thousands of volunteers contributing worldwide on a collaborative work of unprecedented range and participation. Consider that its one-millionth entry in the English language version—filed March 1, 2006, at an unassuming Jordanhill railway station near Glasgow, elicited more than 400 edits by dozens of people within 24 hours of its posting. By August the entry stretched to five printout pages, including such facts as the number who boarded trains here (85,861) and disembarked (94,613), and where it ranked in bustle (1,029th-busiest station in the U.K.).

This experiment in democracy strikes at the crux and bottom line of the *Encyclopaedia Britannica*. For decades considered the apogee of research material, *EB's* thick and musty leather-bound volumes are now CD-ROMs; its most comprehensive edition contains just 120,000 entries. If you want to know about Sudoku, Philadelphia cheese steak, the Rhinoceros Party of Canada, the Gates' family mansion, or the War of the Spanish Succession, you'll have to turn to Wikipedia.

It's not just in span where Wikipedia kicks butt, although its absence of size limits and presence of interested volunteer contributors makes seemingly *anything* Wiki fodder. It's in its ability to jump on the news, to be current, where it really shines. Six hours after Hezbollah militants kidnapped two Israeli soldiers on July 12, 2006, a report found its way here and in the next two weeks was edited more than 4,000 times.

Increasingly it's ordinary civilians, like those who contribute to Wikipedia, who are the first responders to world events. During the London bombing in July 2005, riders on the Underground took the most immediate (and most memorable) photos using their cell phones. And it was lay people, not journalists, who sent in the initial dispatches on the South Asia tsunami in 2004 and Hurricane Katrina in New Orleans in 2005. On a lighter note, want to know anything about any of the dozen finalists on the 2006 season of *American Idol?* You know where you'll need to click.

Not everything is accurate or reliable in what's been described as "a lumpy work in progress" and "the textual equivalent of a film shot with a handheld camera." Unlike such experts in their fields as Einstein, Curie, Mencken, and Houdini solicited by *Britannica, anyone* absorbed by a topic can weigh in on Wikipedia, making for some embarrassing drive-by pranks.

Some tomfoolery involves what's put in; other mischief, what's taken out. Put up to it by their English professor, students at University of South Florida contributed entries for *numpty* ("tea from the land of Nump"), *gavilan* ("a species of left-wing American focused solely on doom and gloom"), and other nonsense words. At the same time, a link to a book attacking McDonald's mysteriously disappeared from the Golden Arches' entry page.

You can find yourself cast as a genius or a goat in Wikipedia, depending on whether friends, enemies, hired guns, or mischief makers clicked the "edit this page" box. In fall 2005, John Seigenthaler Sr., founder of the First Amendment Center at Vanderbilt University and a former aide to Attorney General Robert F. Kennedy, stumbled across a Wikipedia entry on himself that falsely claimed he lived in the USSR, founded a PR firm, and was involved in the assassinations of both Kennedy brothers. After attempts to nab the writer proved fruitless (entries are made anonymously under screen names), Seigenthaler recounted his ordeal at the hands of "a volunteer vandal with poison-pen intellect" in a *USA Today* op-ed. Brian Chase from Nashville eventually fessed up to the hoax, which had gone uncorrected for 132 days.

Politicians have been caught red-handed doctoring their entries and the whole House of Representatives has been banned from Wikipedia at least three times. Sometimes the adjustments are amusing: Senator Robert Byrd's age went from 88 to 180 and Oklahoma Republican Tom Coburn supposedly was voted "most annoying senator" by his peers. Other times they're calculated, with voting records scrubbed to conceal broken campaign promises. Wales himself has been nailed airbrushing his Wikipedia entry—18 times in one year. George W. Bush has been vandalized so often—sometimes more than twice a minute—that W, along with Christina Aguilera and Adolf Hitler, is in Wikipedia's version of the witness protection program. Only people who've registered with the site at least four days earlier can change a semiprotected entry. At times shelter has been granted to Michael Jackson, Shakespeare, John Wayne, sex, food, PlayStation 3, Boston, and God.

Such shenanigans mandated some changes at Wikipedia. Now administrators and robots that police the site for abuse, obscenities, and absurdities can delete offenders, block edits, and revert text in ways ordinary volunteers cannot. An arbitration committee rules on disputes. Guidelines require that content reflect a neutral point of view, be verifiable, and previously published. Wales says, "unending scrutiny and ceaseless editing" from the Wikipedian hive usually corrects initial inaccuracies over time.

From our focus group of two, he's right on. *The Economist* declared Wikipedia's research "surprisingly robust." When *Nature* compared scientific articles from both encyclopedias, it counted four errors in Wikipedia for every three of the meticulously edited, expertly composed *Britannica* (162 vs. 123). That provoked *Britannica* president Jorge Cauz to predict that if his "overzealous," "immature," "fanzine" rival continues without editorial oversight it will "decline into a hulking mediocre mass of uneven, unreliable, and, many times, unreadable articles." For his part, Wales doesn't expect *Britannica* to be around in five years.

Five years before he made that prediction, Wales was struggling to assemble the volunteer online encyclopedia "Nupedia," where experts would edit entries. In one year not even 25 articles had straggled in. Wales had amassed a fortune in a brief stint as an options trader, but had nurtured an open source dream. Influenced by Friedrich Hayek's 1945 free-market manifesto, *The Use of Knowledge in Society*, and H. G. Wells's idealized "world brain," he believed truth would percolate up when people pool their wisdom and continually revise it. And he believed that "truth" should be widely accessible and free. After he heard about "wiki" software, whereby collaborators can easily compose and edit web pages, he shifted direction and opened Wikipedia to everyone. (In Hawaiian, *wiki* means quick.) Within a month of going live on January 15, 2001, Wikipedia had 600 articles; within a year, it had more than 20,000.

More than an encyclopedia or even the poster child of the conflict between digital versus paper or new technology versus traditionalism, or even the representation of consensual truth, Wikipedia is an online community of devotees, a very social, widely scattered but tightly knit hive. Four out of five of the most involved participants are male and they connect with each other passionately around the Wikipedia version of an office cooler.

In some ways, the laboratory that is Wikipedia is like the other popular online communities and social networking sites. Unlike, say, Friendster, MySpace, Facebook, or YouTube, though, Wikipedia doesn't run ads. (It operates on donations.) Spin-offs of it, however, do, like Wikicities, which lets people construct web sites around a common interest, and Wiki24, an unofficial encyclopedia for the TV show 24.

So do cyberhubs like CarSpace.com, where auto buffs congregate to gas about chrome rims or trusted local mechanics, and Dogster.com, Catster.com, Petster.com, and Hamsterster.com, where owners communicate with each other, mainly in the voice of their pets. Many of the online homeowners' grapevines (bulletin boards where neighbors exchange references and anecdotes about plumbers and septic cleaners) also take ads. The for-profit Angie's List, which pulled in more than $12 million in 2006, charges $51 for an annual subscription that includes a local monthly magazine. Ads for the companies reviewed take up about half of each issue.

The most important shopping tool that young, first-time car buyers rely on is MySpace. When Chris DeWolfe bought the URL MySpace.com in 2002, before he was inspired by Friendster to turn it into a friend-connector, he used it to peddle a $99 Chinese E-scooter. When Internet visionary Rupert Murdoch bought it for $580 million in 2005, MySpace had 17 million unique monthly visitors. A year later it had 54 million and was the most visited web site in America.

Some of those visitors were marketers, eager to "befriend" the community to sell them on cell phones, movies, and deodorants. Like regular citizens, these commercial "friends" set up their own pages on MySpace and reach out to touch others in the community. Axe deodorant sponsored a blonde bombshell with the screen name ForBiddeN who claims that 900,000 "friends" link to her MySpace page. Some 75,000 of them signed up to receive Axe's interactive "Gamekillers" based on dating tips. Tower Records, the once great, now defunct music retailer, sent messages (okay, ads) to members interested in hearing about free concerts in their locale. Wendy's created a profile page for the animated square hamburger character from its TV campaign: 100,000 signed on to befriend the square. The trick, marketers know, is to tread carefully so as not to alienate "friends" by polluting their space with overt commercial brandalism.

Recently, in a long, impassioned letter on a popular Internet bulletin board in China, a husband denounced a college student he believed was having an affair with his wife. Tens of thousands of strangers teamed to hound the adulterer out of his university and forced his family to barricade themselves in their home. Cybervigilantism has also dispensed justice for fraud on Internet auction sites and unsolved crimes. Now marketers want to mold the powerful mob mindset that punishes offenders to go on Internet hunts and to embrace and trumpet brands. In the advertising business, we call this social networking, and it's changing the face of advertising.

They recognize the energy (and uncontrollability) of these online communities and some are pandering to them. Beyond a prominent Internet presence, there's often an interactive element to engage consumers with the brand. In 2006, when Planters Peanuts decided its monocled mascot could use an update, it asked the peanut gallery to vote on whether the cane should stay and a pocket watch be added. Old Navy invited the public to select a new spokesdog to succeed Magic.

Some are even inviting audiences to make the ads themselves. In Europe, Sony asked people to refine a TV spot for its Bravia television sets to post on a special web site after an earlier Bravia ad generated a raft of parodies. Current TV, which first handed control of its programming to consumers, now runs ads homemade by them as well.

They're latching on to the appeal of user-generated content and hoping for a bigger boost from buzz marketing, advertising's hottest trend. More than 850 of the nation's largest 1,000 marketers have word-of-mouth programs in gear to penetrate the no-marketing zones people have erected around their lives.

In the academic approach, marketers tap what they call evangelists (rabid fans of a brand) to spread the word about the brand to their social networks. In the practical world, they're praying for a grassroots viral adoption where *anyone* can endorse it to their friends in a cyber-version of the old "telephone-pass-it-on" game by sending along a film clip or ad that caught their fancy, or better yet, in actual face-to-face conversation. McKinsey claims that more than one in every four personal discussions between people includes a discussion of products or services.

Procter & Gamble, a Carat client, pioneered creating online communities around their products. In 2001, it recruited an army of teens (250,000) in the cyber-haunt, Tremor, and then in 2006, a mass of "connector" moms in Vocalpoint (600,000). Their reward for chatting up products: samples, coupons, discounts, first-to-know status, the feeling of being a good (consumerist) Samaritan providing family and friends with valuable information, and the opportunity to be *really* listened to by a company (P&G) dying to hear their opinions.

Although the Tremor crew members aren't told what to say about products and are free to pan or praise them, the world's biggest packaged-goods marketer has come under fire from Commercial Alert. That consumer advocacy group complained to the Federal Trade Commission that Tremor deceives when the "connectors" don't reveal that they're shills. Its executive director, Gary Ruskin, wants the FTC to regulate word-of-mouth (WOM) marketing.

The industry, in the form of the Word of Mouth Marketing Association (WOMMA), already has rules in place, schooled by what happened to e-mail. Lack of self-regulation in the early days led to spam and a black eye for e-mail marketing, technology that blocked marketing messages indiscriminately, and federal anti-spam legislation. WOMMA wants paid recommenders to reveal what they're up to. Transparency is a good thing, it argues (and we agree), pointing to a Northeastern University study that found that rather than being turned off when told they are the subjects of WOM campaign, people were *more* likely to mention the experience to someone else.

Beyond the Wiki clones—ShopWiki.com, and Amazon's ProductWikis, WikiTravel.com, and World66.com (which sell ads for products related to a consumer's search), and Congresspedia.com and scientists' peer-reviewed Encyclopedia of Earth (which don't)— Wikipedia (or at least the premises of active participation, social interaction, and collaboration it champions) has slipped into the corporate conference room. What the young and wired knew from their personal experiences on the Live Web, they're now bringing into the business arena, threatening the old-world command-and-control mentality. Companies like Disney and Dresdner Kleinwort Wasserstein use wikis to get teams to work on the proverbial same page. Others call on social networking services like LinkedIn Corp. and Visible Path Corp. to find employees and customers from the collective contacts of colleagues. "Now that everybody knows what Wikipedia is, it's no stretch for them to imagine a company Wikipedia," says Ross Mayfield, CEO of the corporate wiki outfit Socialtext Inc.

The *open-source* aspect has been adopted (sometimes grudgingly) by mainstream technology companies like AOL, Sun Microsystems, and even mighty Microsoft (to save themselves from open-source alternatives). In three years, the Firefox web browser crept up on Microsoft and now its market share hovers around 14 percent in America and 20 percent in parts of Europe. Searchers on Google, shoppers at Amazon, and traders on eBay rely on open-source software—products that are often built by volunteers and cost nothing to use. More than two out of every three web sites are hosted using open-source Apache. The term has expanded beyond software development to legal research to biotechnology. There's even an open-source initiative to develop drugs to treat diseases in poor countries.

Meanwhile, Wikipedia is shepherding volunteers in compiling a Wiktionary and a Wikiquote, with definitions and quotations in many languages, and Wikibooks school texts to be freely given as gifts. Based on their encyclopedia parent, they, too, will probably be patchy and in some places thin, though they should lurch toward perfection with more chefs stirring the brew. (An open-source adage maintains that "given enough eyeballs, all bugs are shallow.")

Wikipedia never claimed absolute validity or omniscience. It could rightly have claimed to be a Darwinian process by which a first draft evolves into something better, an enormous and inviting reservoir from which to sip cautiously, the embodiment of the Web's potential and a roadmap for knowledge creation. All in all, it is a spectacular invention, don't you think?

10

WHY A KILLER VIDEO GAME
IS THE U.S. ARMY'S BEST
RECRUITMENT TOOL

Since the last draftee reported for duty in December 1972, Uncle Sam has had to hustle to staff an all-volunteer armed force. In the case of the U.S. Army, that meant recruiting 80,000 new soldiers every year—essentially replacing more than the entire workforce of BellSouth every 12 months.

Advertising did the trick initially. After "Today's Army Wants to Join You" fizzled, in January 1981, "Be All You Can Be" became the battle cry. For two decades, wrapped around ads that made this branch look as adventurous as an Outward Bound course, it resonated with 17-to-24-year-olds (of whom the Army is the nation's largest employer). Then, in 2001, that was scuttled for an "Army of One." ("Even though there are 1,045,690 soldiers just like me, I am my own force. . . .") Critics scoffed that the new tin slogan was misguided (isn't conformity more valued than individuality in the barracks?); the Army countered that it was effective.

Then Iraq exploded.

Despite adding thousands of additional recruiters, upping the enlistment bonus and funding for college, fattening the ad budget, and ratcheting up the patriotic appeal, the Army could not fill its boots.

So the Army added more marketing weaponry. It hosted town hall meetings where civilians could meet soldiers and hear about their accomplishments. It tried product placement: Army mechanics on the Discovery Channel's *Monster Garage* tricked out a Jeep. And it launched a thoroughly engaging computer video game that quickly became a gold standard of "advergames" for its effectiveness and realism. Gamers take such real military roles as Intelligence (18F), Engineer (18C), Communications (18E), and Combat Medic (18D), and fire the same weapons the Army has. And when they fire on the run, their aim is less accurate.

Before it was released on July 4, 2002, many expected the $7.3 million game would join the ranks of the $436 hammer and $640 toilet seat as a study of excess. Few predicted "America's Army" would become the artillery's most effective marketing tool, conveying the authentic military experience in a voice that prospective recruits want to hear.

More than seven million users have registered (anonymously so as to squelch any fear of recruiter harangues) with 10,000 to 50,000 new ones downloading the shoot-em-up daily. In a dozen running and gunning missions, players advance through the stages of soldierhood—drilling in basic training, target practicing with an M-16, learning about basic emergency medicine, and, finally, diving into combat. The game has been downloaded more than 16 million times, 20 percent of entering cadets at West Point have played it, and between 20 and 40 percent of new Army recruits have played it as well.

"They seek it out rather than the other way around," noted Chris Chambers, deputy director of the Army Game Project within the Army's Office of Economic and Manpower Analysis. At an average cost of 10 cents per hour versus $5 to $10 per hour for a TV commercial, it delivers immersion rather than mere impression.

"America's Army" has proven to be such powerful weaponry that an official game store does brisk business selling collectible action figures, clothes, coffee mugs, and other doodads emblazoned with the logo. The Army builds parties and tournaments across the country around it. A wireless version and sequels including "America's Army: Special Forces," where players try to earn a Green Beret by completing Special Forces missions, have been released. Apple created a knockoff: Boot Camp. And the Army now even uses it extensively in training.

Uncle Sam Wants You . . . to play . . . and he's not the only one. *Everyone* is getting in on the virtual action. Some, like the Army, create a whole game that functions as a sales brochure. Just as the Army promoted its pro-military message through gameplay, the United Nations World Food Program aims to educate about its mission to combat hunger worldwide. In "Food Force," players steer a helicopter over the war-torn island of Sheylan, (a fictional cross between Sri Lanka and Somalia) and drop relief supplies to a population with little shelter and less food. Or they create food rations, schedule shipments, or take a supply truck through hostile terrain.

In the racing game, "Volvo Drive for Life" (playable on Microsoft's Xbox), players are rewarded not for finishing first, but for avoiding accidents. Wander in for a test drive at a Volvo dealer and you can try it in the showroom. Dealers can bestow game cartridges on select prospects and customers. After its royal mascot tromped through "Fight Night Round 3" (on Xbox 360), Burger King created action games around its bizarre king and made them available for just $3.99 to customers who bought a value meal. (Most games sell for at least 12 times that). Nike went beyond athletes wearing its shoes in the video game NBA 2K6: Tournament players are given different pairs of virtual footwear and choose which to put on from their Nike shoe locker depending on the task. They can also personalize the shoes with the same customization feature that's on Nike's iD web site.

In other advergames, marketers hitch a ride. In "CSI: 3 Dimensions of Murder," Visa's fraud-monitoring capabilities shine when a suspicious charge on a victim's credit card triggers investigation by a forensic-sciences team. In Tom Clancy's "Splinter Cell Chaos Theory," the protagonist, secret agent Sam Fisher, scales a bright neon sign for Axe deodorant and quietly enters a lunchroom inhabited by a Diet Sprite Zero vending machine. (Axe also created Mojo Master, an online game about picking up women.) In "Splinter Cell: Pandora Tomorrow," Fisher retrieves a message from a Sony Ericsson smart phone to learn who the villain is. In "Burnout Revenge," players drive and crash a Carl's Jr. delivery-truck. And players in Activision's

"True Crime" titles take a break from fighting gangs to recover stolen Puma sneakers.

Some marketers install games on corporate web sites or designated URLs, like "Life Saver Candy Stand," or FiletoFish.com, the web site where a division of McDonald's posted "Shark Bait" (in English and Spanish). Players must protect the filet-of-fish sandwich from attacking sharks. For Wachovia, Carat's Fusion recreated the tricky 17th-hole par 3 at the Quail Hollow Club in Charlotte, North Carolina. Players evaluate distance and wind conditions on this 217-yard hole to pick a club: Crowd noise lets them know if they've made a good virtual swing. Wachovia has sponsored the annual PGA championship since 2002: The game was fashioned to promote that, sell tickets, and create viral buzz. H&R Block's "Deduct-A-Buck" game at the deductabuck.com web site is tax-time seasonal. Players who correctly answer questions about what they can legally write off in this Seventies-TV-quiz-show-style game win prizes.

Hollywood and Nashville hardly launch a movie or song anymore without serving up a side of game. And despite hefty royalty rates for movie titles, an action hit will almost certainly be reincarnated on a console. Turner's "Witchblade" promoted the TV series, and games built around *Men in Black II*, *Spider-Man*, and *Crocodile Hunter: Collision Course* were meant to promote the new releases. Along with ads for Sprite , the sci-fi game "Planetside" featured ads for the movie *Deuce Bigalow: European Gigolo*, and in the free version of "Anarchy Online" a 15-second trailer for *V for Vendetta* played in a continual loop. Ads for *Batman Begins* in "Splinter Cell" were timed to its release in local markets.

The Da Vinci Code got its own PS2 game. Paramount Pictures crafted a *Mission: Impossible III* game for cell phones while *Miami Vice* had an accompanying game to play on Sony's handheld PSP.

This is about more than fun and games. Yankee Group estimates that by 2007 a serious gamer will lurk in every fourth home in America. Nielsen says three out of four residences with guys under age 34 have a game system. More people slay orcs in the medieval-style quest for virtual gold and power, "World of Warcraft," than live in Denmark. In 2006, gamers across the globe owned more than 100 million PlayStation2s and 40 million Xboxes. In the United States, video games already raked in more money than the movie box offices, and Yankee Group says the industry will top $8.3 billion by 2008. PricewaterhouseCoopers says globally it will reach $55 billion by 2009. That explains why a cottage industry in Los Angeles builds game consoles into the backs of Lincoln Navigators.

Collectively, interactive ads embedded in quizzes and games made up more than $1 billion of the $12.5 billion in online ad revenue in 2005, according to the Interactive Advertising Bureau. Nielsen (which now measures the industry) expects advertising spending within games will jump from $75 million in 2006 to $1 billion by 2010. Mitch Davis, CEO of Massive, thinks it could be almost twice that—and account for about 3 percent of all media spending, just shy of what advertisers spend on the Internet.

Microsoft must think so, too. In spring 2006, it bought Massive Inc. with hopes of linking its in-game ad placement network with Microsoft's own ad-brokering unit, AdCenter, to give Google real competition. Massive, like Double Fusion Inc., IGA Worldwide Inc., and Atom Entertainment Inc., places ads for clothes, beverages, films, and music on more than 100 console games. Davis founded Massive in 2002 after becoming disoriented by a fake clothing ad for Gup (a takeoff of Gap) he saw while playing "Grand Theft Auto: Vice City." Real ads would add a sense of realism, he decided, and it would add a revenue stream to a nascent industry.

Who plays? Young guys, of course, but not just them; research suggests that investment bankers and their ilk, education- and incomewise, are the norm. "Warcraft" has become the new golf as young businessmen assemble online here rather than on greens at country clubs.

There are some girl-games too: Kimberly-Clark's "KT's Impossi-Bubble Adventures" never mentions tampons as girls try to prevent their snarky brothers from reading their diaries. After they're done playing they're invited to a page that discusses it. And a new crop of brain-food video games hit the market recently, aimed at boomers, including word and number puzzles like Sudoku, connect-the-dots exercises, and other timed challenges. Gamers spend considerably less time watching TV and movies, because of this recently discovered passion. Volvo figures its target audience spends 8 to 13 hours a week gaming.

Perhaps surprisingly, they actually welcome real ads (as opposed to generic ones for fake products) in these environments—especially if they subsidize playtime—because they create a more authentic experience. That means the ads must blend in so an avatar (online persona) walking past a storefront in a virtual city could spy TVs inside running a video ad, or, while joysticking around a digital Los Angeles in "American Wasteland," innocently cross paths with 3-D Jeep Wranglers, Grand Cherokees, and Liberties.

Feedback after DaimlerChrysler got in the game suggests why other marketers want to play. Dodge was able to pump up awareness of, and interest in, its cars among Internet users who played "Race the Pros" while dodging rules that prevent it from touting speed in TV ads. Engage with pro skateboarder Tony Hawk's video game for 20 minutes and you'll have seen Jeeps, on average, 23 times. Ninety-six percent of players remembered them and felt they fit unobtrusively enough that two out of three would consider buying one when they needed new wheels. Chrysler's marketing team determined that gaming works far better than TV ads to turn brand awareness into an actual preference.

There is a downside, of course: Advertisers like Airwaves chewing gum were flamed for "hiding their subliminal messages in plain sight" in "Splinter Cell: Chaos Theory." Postings on fan web site HalfLife2.net likened ads in gaming to "telemarketing ringing up while you're having dinner." A blogger wailed that it's right up there in the history of bad marketing ideas with "tobacco execs saying cigarettes aren't addictive." And there's been some foul play: Engage In-Game Advertising inserted ads for Subway's $2.49 daily specials on billboards in "Counter-Strike" war zones without permission from the game's publisher.

For now at least, the benefits outweigh the brickbats. Nielsen research found that gamers remember the ads on average 2.5 times better than viewers recall TV commercials. And not only is it less costly on a CPM or cost-per-participant basis, but there's also a lot less waste. The game's sweet spot, young men, comprise just 37 percent of TV network audiences compared with 65 percent of video-gamers. Marketers are also more involved in how their ads are placed in the gamescape, or digital architecture. Ford didn't know until Fox's 24 was shot how its cars would look on screen, but Chrysler weighed in on how its cars would play in "American Wasteland." (All games' creative developers green-light ads only if they don't interfere with game play, functionality, or bandwidth. The nation's leading game-maker, Electronic Arts, which pioneered game placements with McDonald's and Intel in 2002, rejected them when launching "Sims 2 Open for Business," because the game's design staff decided it would detract from the player's experience.) The two million brand-placement dollars that Activision took in from Chrysler, Nokia, and Motorola offset 10 percent of "American Wasteland's" development costs.

Marketers are also enthralled by the dynamic way their ads are embedded. Instead of hard-coded as static ads, they can change. Massive, for one, pushes specific ads to predetermined zip codes, demographics, time zones, or other variables. A pizza ad, say, would materialize on a billboard at 8 P.M., rather than at 8 A.M.

And they like the dynamic way the ads unfold. To promote its DVD video camera, Panasonic turned to Funcom's free, futuristic alien battle MMO game "Anarchy Online." (MMOG means massively multiplayer online game, where hundreds of thousands of players from around the world compete against each other at the same time.) Its ad begins as the player's alter-ego approaches a billboard or screen that's scenery on the street and gets louder as the character nears the ad. He can stop and "watch" or walk on by. The next time he passes the ad, it picks up right where he stopped watching, until he's seen the full 15-second spot.

Sony's fantasy role-playing game, "Everquest," which has about 300,000 players, has gone even further. Forget about speed dialing. A player can type "pizza" to open a browser window and order home delivery from Pizza Hut. The official site invites players to "just kick back until fresh pizza is delivered straight to your door."

And game designers are enthralled by what the all-seeing ad-tracking system offers. Character interactions with ads are tracked immediately. So, if a character is stumped in front of an ad, its creators realize that the mission or level is too difficult.

Marketers have been playing with games for a long time. Back in the Neanderthal 1980s, "Teenage Mutant Ninja Turtles" promoted a pizza chain in an arcade game. In 1999, GlaxoSmithKline borrowed *Tomb Raider* icon Lara Croft to help sell its energy drink, Lucozade, on TV. It even changed the beverage's name temporarily to Larazade. In the spot, designed to transform it as a drink for the sick to a drink for fitness, the animated cyberbabe is about to be dismembered by a chainsaw-wielding brute. The words GAME PAUSED appear, the video game player leaves the room, and Lara and her nemesis sit back and relax with a bottle of Lucozade. The game player returns and the action picks up where it left off.

Then, in 2001, to promote Steven Spielberg's *A.I.*, Dreamworks and Warner Bros. green-lighted what's now recognized as the first-ever alternate reality game (ARG). While aside from a few crossover characters it had little to do with the actual film, it aimed to establish a parallel plot and sketch out the universe in "A.I." Players had to puzzle out why a character named Evan Chan was murdered by finding clues in such diverse, arcane areas as Italian futurist paintings and 16th-century French lute tablature and collaborating with other online sleuths. By the time the game ended, more than a million problem-solvers had taken part.

Another dimension that intrigues advertisers is that the games spawn connected communities. Fantasy leagues of cyberathletes have sprung up, sponsored by soda and snack companies. Craig Levine, founder of E-Sports Entertainment, figures that between 3,500 and 4,000 fantasy teams were created in the most recently concluded fantasy e-sports league season. Their tournaments are covered by MTV. There's even a Cyberathlete Professional League sponsored by AMD, ATI, Pizza Hut, Verizon, and others.

In "The Beast," as the "A.I." game came to be known, players phoned and faxed each other and knitted together so closely that managers wondered what it could teach about office teamwork. And when the fictitious character Jamie Kane, of the fictitious boy-band Boy*d Upp, died in a helicopter crash en route to a video shoot, his real-life fans made sure it was reported by the BBC and appeared (albeit briefly) in Wikipedia. Neither "The Beast" nor those caught up in it recognized any game boundaries.

Increasingly games are moving beyond virtual boundaries. The retailer Champs Sports stamps its logo on the helmets of Electronic Arts' "Arena Football" virtual athletes and its "Where sport lives" signage at the end zone. Within Champs' 600 real-world stores, monitors show the game, employees are rewarded with cartridges as sales incentives, and kiosks invite shoppers to have a go at it and win Champs merchandise.

When Audi launched its new Audi A3 in 2005, it opened "The Art of the Heist" with TV, newspaper, radio, and magazine ads, billboards, on-line banners, a microsite, wild postings and blogs, live events nationwide, and an online "Bourne Identity Meets The Da Vinci Code" thriller sleuth game. Hit men are pursuing Nisha Roberts, an expert art retriever, her tech-wiz boyfriend, Ian Yarborough, and famous game designer Virgil Tatum. While racing for their lives (cross-country in an A3, naturally), they must foil an intended art heist. The mission engaged more than 200,000 people in a single day and 500,000 on an ongoing basis, sparked online buzz, caused traffic to audiusa.com to spike, resulted in the creation of seven fan sites, and generated thousands of leads. Audi ad director Stephen Berkov compared it to a jet engine "sucking people into the intake."

Actually, ARGs seem more like falling down rabbit holes with their surrealistic blend of factual events with the imaginings of both the game creators and players. Perhaps the online virtual world conjured in the MMOG game "Second Life" most embodies this. "Residents" (as they call themselves) roam endless land- and cityscapes, hang with friends, conduct business, brew cups of tea, savor a soft breeze, hear a fountain gurgle, and build idealized homes on plots of imaginary land represented by pixels on the computer screens. But these imaginary characters are generating very real money. The game's currency, "Linden dollars" (named for its production company), can convert into U.S. dollars (at about 250 to the real dollar, though they fluctuate) through a credit card transaction at an online currency exchange. Stranger than fiction, some 3,100 residents earned a net profit of more than $20,000 (real U.S. bucks) in 2006 from their "Second Life" enterprises. One of them, Chris Mead, sells more than 300 cute animation balls that unfold into couples dancing and cuddling at around $1 each, to clear $1,900 a week. And the online sci-fi game "Entropia Universe" issued a real-world ATM card so its 250,000 players could withdraw real dollars converted from their Project Entropia Dollars or PEDs (at 10 to a U.S. dollar).

Money isn't all players can take away from these new-world playgrounds. Economists regard these unregulated virtual worlds as ideal testing grounds for new ideas.British branding firm Rivers Run Red has teamed real-world fashion firms with denizens of "Second Life" to create and showcase new designs. Corporate training teams from Wal-Mart, American Express, Intel, and 200 other companies have come together under the aegis of think tank The MASIE Center in Saratoga Springs, New York, to experiment inside "Second Life" with ways for companies to act more collaboratively. They are studying the incentive systems within "Second Life," the hive mind, what appeals work, and the gamers' psychology to see what can be imported into our real-world economy.

Our next frontiers are not on the edges of the solar system. They're in the cyberworld, with video games as the portal.

11

WHY HOWARD STERN IS
EARNING SIRIUS MONEY

O n February 28, 2006, when CBS sued Howard Stern, his
company, One Twelve, his agent, and that agent's firm, Don
Buchwald & Associates, along with Sirius Satellite Radio for
multiple breaches of contract, fraud, unjust enrichment, and
misappropriation of broadcast time to promote his new gig, a lot more
was at stake than sour grapes. The "Tiffany" network, indeed, all terrestrial radio, was battling a new, onerous celestial force that the heavens
seemed to unleash upon it like a modern-day plague.

Here was yet another pestilence to endure for an 85-year-old industry lately beset by them. *Everyone* listens to radio—230 million Americans
are habitués—and the medium rakes in more than $20 billion in annual
advertising revenue, counting national advertising and the 297 spot markets. But the traditional or terrestrial kind grew only 1.5 percent in 2005.
The time consumers spend with radio has dropped sharply, too, according to Arbitron, as listeners play with their iPods, cell phones, and other
new toys. Stern's P. T. Barnum–like exit from traditional radio wasn't just
like Michael Jordan retiring from the NBA; it was like Darth Vader cross-
ing over to the dark side.

The fearless bad boy of radio, who spews whatever he thinks (or
thinks his audience wants him to think) with no restraint, hawked his

new gig so often in his waning days at CBS that he was ultimately forced to replace the verboten name "Sirius" with "Uh-uh." Rather than confuse his fans, that tightened the bond, making them feel like insiders in Stern's cabal. *Advertising Age* estimated his Sirius plugs in the first 40 minutes of his October 20 broadcast were worth $1.2 million in free ad time. CBS could have chucked Stern early, but he was lining their coffers and soon enough they'd have to deal with the day that he no longer did.

That day came on January 9, 2006, when Stern's new satellite show bounced into the stratosphere. It took just 21 minutes in his new studio for Stern to utter his first *f*-word. Beyond the reach of the Federal Communications Commission and their pesky "content restrictions," Stern unleashed his resident "wackpackers" of farters, strippers, and porn stars along with obscenities, sexual sounds, and scatological jokes. The Family Media Guide counted 740 curse words (including 77 instances of the *f*-word). And America's number-one shock jock, who'd brought the first networked/syndicated AM show to music radio in the 1980s, was turning his bile on the "boring, old-fashioned" and "overcommercialized" venue he'd rejected.

CBS's initial attempt to plug the hole that Stern left with former Van Halen frontman David Lee Roth in New York and Adam Carolla on the West Coast fizzled. Its Los Angeles–based KLSX went from number one in morning drive time to not even among the top 20 among full-signal commercial FM stations. Roth did even worse, and in less than three months was out of a job. His replacements, Opie and Anthony, did a lot better, according to the Arbitron spring 2006 ratings survey. Foulmouthed talkers on the *other* satellite radio, XM, Opie and Anthony had been fired by CBS in 2002 after they broadcast live (via cell phone) a couple having sex in New York's St. Patrick's Cathedral. The duo (really Gregg Hughes and Anthony Cumia) do three hours each weekday on CBS and another two hours on XM. CBS anticipated that it could take two years to replace the $100 million that Stern contributed to its bottom line from the 27 stations that carried him.

Meanwhile, Stern was relentlessly plugging to generate subscriptions (at $12.95 a month) for Sirius. From October 2004, when he signed on, until he moved into his new studio, subscriptions quintupled to 3.3 million, revenue more than tripled, and the value of Sirius stock jumped. (Stern had more than $200 million in financial incentives to pump up those numbers.)

This was progress, for sure, but nowhere near the 12 million to 15 million who listened to his old show. One unlikely beneficiary of the diaspora is National Public Radio. Many who won't pay to follow Stern have gravitated to NPR. Its political orientation is centrist-leftist in a drive-time dominated by conservatives, and like Stern, it specializes in quirky, offbeat takes on the news.

But for all the gains, Sirius is bleeding red. Pay radio has never made money. In 2005, Sirius lost $863 million on revenues of $242 million. (Banc of America Securities analyst Jonathan Jacoby estimates Stern cost Sirius close to $670 million.) XM, with six million customers paying at $10 to $12 a month, was down $667 million on revenues of $558 million. Both expect to be solvent by 2007 and each expects to have added at least three million subscribers, for a total of more than 15 million, by then. Kagan Research forecasts that 44 million will subscribe by 2010 and 46.8 million by 2014. And despite illicit downloading, widely available bootlegged versions on the Net, and pirate radio stations rebroadcasting the shows on unclaimed FM radio frequencies, Kagan expects they'll generate $7.6 billion in revenue by then. (Many consider that overblown, noting that, combined, Sirius and XM nationwide are smaller than the Chicago market.)

The key is in the car. Every automaker is installing satellite radio as standard equipment in the 16-to-17-million new cars Americans buy every year—and giving the buyer the first year's subscription free. They get a chunk of the renewal fee and a new after-market revenue stream. "Ford makes more money on the revenue share from satellite radio than it does selling cars," boasts Sirius chief executive, Mel Karmazin.

The "taste" is addictive, says Karmazin. Subscribers spend 86 percent of their radio time tuned to Sirius. On its 125 stations (including one in

Korean, another in German, and one from Martha Stewart) they can lis-ten to any football game anywhere and customize what they want to hear: the Patriot game, for example, narrated by the team's own commen-tator. "If they want, they can block out Howard talking penises," says Karmazin. Sirius subscribers could get the Playboy Channel free if they activated it. Four weeks after Stern talked it up, 500,000 listeners had done so. XM's big drawers are Major League Baseball, NASCAR, and Oprah Winfrey, who "is to women what sports is to men," says XM chief executive, Hugh Panero.

Because listeners' top objection to terrestrial radio is its surfeit of ads, Karmazin plans to keep commercials between 10 and 30 percent of Sir-ius's revenues. Music channels are ad-free, but Stern's daily show could soon include nine minutes of ads on each of its five hours, at around $6,500 for a prerecorded ad, and $15,000 or more for a live read. That's roughly what CBS charged for fewer than half the listeners.

One reason is that "in our pre-arrogant days we're trying unusual for-mats," says Karmazin. "If an advertiser wants a 10-second ad or a whole channel, we're talking," he says. Tanqueray, for example, ran a two-and-a-half-minute spot. Another is that the audience is overall more affluent and better educated than the norm. And Stern—whether you see him as a gross pervert or a martyr for free speech—attracts a broad audience. Pay-ing for radio rankles even the devotees, but surveys indicate 75 percent of satellite radio subscribers are highly satisfied. Both services lose less than 2 percent of their subscribers a month, and every advertiser who bought Stern's show has stayed, gloats Karmazin.

That's impressive when you consider all the other ways to get com-mercial-free music: from cell phone subscription-based radio services like Motorola's iRadio or Sprint Nextel's clone, Apple's iPod, and everyone's podcast. USC Media Lab found that 85 percent of 18-to-24-year-olds would rather listen to music from their MP3 players or over the Net than traditional radio.

Cell phones *have* taken a bite out of traditional radio. Bridge Ratings found that cell phone–equipped commuters who drive at least an hour a day listen to radio less (26 minutes today instead of 32 in 2003) and chat on their phones more (13.49 minutes a day from 10.45 minutes a day in

2003). Driving must make people talkative. They make longer calls behind the wheel than otherwise: on average, 4 minutes and 21 seconds
compared with the overall average cell phone call lasting 3 minutes and
15 seconds.

Terrestrial radio has stopped playing possum. Beyond CBS going after Howard's end, they're going digital and offering new services. Airline
pilots taking off from Miami International Airport often get an earful of
hip-hop tunes from radio station Da Streetz, which edged onto a treach-
erously narrow band. Radio interference—hisses, whistles, static, blurred
or no reception—is now common on AM as larger stations transition to
the better digital broadcasts and interfere with the analog signals of their
next-door neighbors on the dial. High-definition radio, which can give
an AM station the same quality sound of an FM and FM the same quality
as a CD, allows for text scrolling and all its advertising ramifications. It
also lets broadcasters split their signals and squeeze up to three additional
channels on the same frequency formerly occupied by one. (That means
markets without country, oldies, or gospel, for example, can get them. It
also means that big radio owners are trolling for content. Clear Channel,
for example, developed a new content and programming R&D division.
One initiative named "Project 75" resulted in the development of 75 new
formats subdivided into 400 niche programming types.) Only 10 kilohertz separates each AM station on the dial versus 200 kilohertz between
each FM station.

Things will get a lot fuzzier before they crystallize. In 2006, just
700 of the 4,757 AM and 8,903 FM stations in the United States had
added digital signals. By 2007, their numbers will have doubled, and
the receivers, with TiVo-like functionality that lets the owner store and
replay, will cost half what they did in 2006. (A temporary boon: The
FCC currently makes AM broadcasters switch off their digital trans-
mission at night when AM radio signals are more erratic, to cut back
on side interference.)

Because listeners are getting so much of their music elsewhere, terrestrial radio upped the amount of talk it offers. The number of stations offering news/talk has rocketed to 1,988 in June 2006 with niches for
female talk, hot talk, and sports talk, for example. And more stations be-

gan broadcasting in Spanish—Inside Radio Database Princeton charts the growth from 665 commercial stations in 2004 to 708 in 2005 as a result of the surge in population of Spanish speakers and their newly recognized buying clout.

Many have embraced Jack, an amorphous new format imported from Canada. Jack stations have no deejay or set genre: They mix tunes from different eras without transitions. Listeners never know what's next. It seems to work: According to *Billboard*, 12 of the 18 top market stations that flipped to Jack recently saw dramatically improved ratings.

Terrestrials are also punching back by touting their cost to consumers—zilch—and to advertisers—effective. Arbitron, the rating service for radio, has moved beyond diaries listeners kept to pager-sized Portable People Meters that provide minute-by-minute listening reads to more accurately reflect audiences. Houston's International Demographics and partner Ipsos of France developed a smart cell phone that electronically measures behavior of radio listeners by picking up an encoded signal. Did you stop at IHOP after hearing the ad say that you were approaching it? We'll soon know the answer.

Some terrestrial stations have even cut the number of ads they run to become more attractive to listeners as well as advertisers. Collectively the stations in the top 10 markets across the nation devoted 7.7 percent less airtime for commercials in December 2005 than they did in December 2004, according to media analyst Leland Westerfield at Harris Nesbitt bank. Most of this is because the radio leader, Clear Channel, intentionally shaved two minutes of ad time each hour (from 10 minutes and 46 seconds down to 8 minutes and 44 seconds) as part of its Less is More campaign to push up ad rates and lure back alienated listeners. It did the trick: Adult listenership increased 7 percent over the summer of 2005.

Perhaps terrestrial radio's most aggressive tactic is moving beyond the tall towers in big fields to go online—and interactive. The first music video ever aired—the Buggles' "Video Killed the Radio Star" on MTV on August 1, 1981—was hardly prophetic; co-opted would have been closer to the truth. ABC News Radio Networks has had a subscription-based, audio-on-demand web site for talk host Sean Hannity since November 2004, and is making all of its radio content available online for station affiliates on demand. In 2006, Clear Channel had a music video on-demand service through 16 station web sites—and the mechanism to sell downloadable songs—to take on all comers including music sites like Yahoo! Music, AOL Radio Network, and Urge, MTV's Internet music service developed with Microsoft. In 2006, Clear Channel had 450 stations that played online music live: An average of 860,900 listeners logged onto it each week. The videos are free to visitors but they must first watch a 15-second ad.

They've also been aggressive podcasters. What began as free, grassroots, ad-free rantings has been corporatized. Amateur hour still abounds: So many churches use podcasts to communicate that it's been dubbed Godcasting. (The podcast page at yahoo.com offers more than 36,000 downloads in the religion category.) But since March 2006, when Ricky Gervais, star of *The Office*, began charging $2 for each comedic podcast (generating 250,000 downloads a week from Apple's iTunes Music Store), radio stations have been podcasting their programming. *Billboard Radio Monitor* found that 19 FM stations in the top markets offer some level of podcasting or downloadable audio content. Premiere Radio Networks offers subscriptions for podcasts from seven personalities, including Rush Limbaugh and Dr. Laura Schlessinger, as well as a free, sponsored podcast version of *American Top 40 With Ryan Seacrest*. CNN Radio has five weekly podcasts including a weekly NASCAR report. Radio Disney aims its ad-supported podcasts at the young kids, and ESPN podcasts snippets with the hope listeners like what they hear and tune into more on terrestrial radio.

There were more than 16,000 different podcasts available online, 1,000 times more than were available just 18 months earlier. According to Bridge Research, nine million people now listen to podcasts, and by 2010, 12 million should be in the fold. EMarketer expects podcast advertising spending to rocket from $80 million in 2006 to $300 million by 2010. Venture capitalist Sequoia Capital thinks it can reach $2 billion by 2011. The next radio receptor that networks and stations are eyeing is the cell phone. In March 2006, NPR began delivering podcasts to mobile phones, and Clear Channel has been talking to carriers about doing so for a year.

Now that satellite has shocked terrestrial into getting into high gear, what will radio be in 2010? No doubt it will be a scrollable, narrowcasted, healthy medium that provides an earful to listeners and a good way for advertisers to reach them.

12

WHY OPRAH GAVE
AWAY PONTIACS

P
ope Benedict XVI wears Bushnell Performance Optics' Serengeti-
branded sunglasses, brown walking shoes by Geox, or sometimes
stylish red loafers believed to be Pradas, and toys with his white
Apple iPod Nano. As the spiritual leader of more than one billion
Catholics, the pontiff can't endorse anything but doctrine. That, however,
hasn't stopped a mass of companies from pursuing pope-and-product jux-
tapositions by sending their goods to the Holy See to be seen. But another
spiritual leader not only can be seen with products, she can openly champion them, and she has something the pope doesn't: a hugely popular
talk-show.

In autumn 1994, when Pontiac was launching its G6, a record 65
other new car models were debuting—11 times more than that of a
decade earlier. Facing that kind of competition gridlock, General Motors
knew it had only a six-month window before it would have to resort to
rebates and risk its Pontiac G6 being stigmatized as distressed merchandise. So it turned to Oprah.

GM tried to interest the daytime diva in featuring the car on her "My
Favorite Things" episode. Oprah's team suggested that Pontiac give one
to all 276 members of her studio audience—an expenditure that easily

surpassed three 30-second commercials in that year's Super Bowl. This was a lot to swallow.

But they ponied up the Pontiacs and got a spokesperson trusted by millions. Oprah devoted nearly the entire September 13, 2004 show to lauding the G6, touring an assembly plant and promoting its On-Star, satellite radio, and quality-control features. When she leaped up shouting "Everybody gets a car!" women screamed, men cried, and they all raced to the parking lot to ogle their new, fully-loaded wheels.

Soon after that blockbuster, Pontiac was on a roll. Regis and Kelly handed out keys to a Pontiac Montana SV6 minivan each weekday for a month. Nine survivors of *Survivor* got cars. In 2005, one of the tasks on *The Apprentice* was producing a marketing brochure for Pontiac's Solstice roadster.

The results were interesting. Despite the $20 million worth of awareness generated, even Oprah could not prevent the G6 from gathering dust on dealers' lots. But more interesting than that in our minds was how Detroit went to Tinseltown to put drivers behind their wheels.

Pontiac is in heavy traffic on the product-placement highway. One reason is that entertainment companies sell the same space to different advertisers for film in theaters, on network TV, basic cable, and DVD. That means that the cars Jack Bauer drives can be and are changed within the same exact scene—a sort of vehicular body double. In DVDs of 24, Bauer and his colleague Chloe each drove Toyotas, while villains careened around in other makes. In the made-for-TV version, Bauer is never too far from his Ford Expedition. A greater emotional connection than Bauer's counterterrorism ops came when Claire Fisher got behind the wheel of a Toyota Prius in the series finale of *Six Feet Under*. Her long drive from California to New York was filled with visions of her loved ones' deaths. And how do you think the editorial idea for a piece in *Playboy* on "The best way to make love in a Mini" (with diagrams using crash-test dummies) arose?

Sometimes it seems make and model get enough screentime to share hero billing. If they were people, Ferrari Testarossa would be on line cashing royalty checks for its role on *Miami Vice* right behind DeLorean Coyote from *Hardcastle & McCormick*. The Dodge Charger has become virtually synonymous with *Dukes of Hazzard* and is fast approaching icon status. Chrysler Jeeps are the auto of choice for Laura Croft, Tomb Raider.

And while the BMW Z8 and DeLorean were integral to *The World Is Not Enough* and *Back to the Future* respectively, Audi didn't just place a car in *I, Robot* for its star turn in 2004. It created the RSQ concept car specifically for the futuristic action film.

But perhaps no automaker has had more supporting roles (product placements) than Ford. Its cars were cast in almost half of the films that topped the weekly box office in 2005 (19 out of 41 movies). The Mustang Cobra was almost Charlie's fourth Angel, and where would *Starsky & Hutch* be without their Grand Torino?

Then there's Pixar-animated personalities of various models in *Cars*. The speedy but arrogant hero, Lightning McQueen (a Corvette voiced by Owen Wilson), gets sidetracked from the racing circuit in wayward Radiator Springs where a hippie 1960 Volkswagen bus (voiced by George Carlin) brews his own "organic fuel," and the 1959 Chevy Impala is Ramone, the low rider (comedian Cheech Marin). In this world where cars live and breathe, hotels serve Lincoln Continental breakfast and insects are winged VW bugs.

You need only open your eyes to see brand cameos knitted into film and TV shows, magazines, videogames, and music—so many that PQ Media calculated the market's worth at $3.6 billion in 2005. Nielsen figures the time devoted to them rose 21 percent just from 2004 to 2005. CBS chief Leslie Moonves expects that three-fourths of all scripted prime-time network shows will soon contain paid product placement.

We have no one but ourselves to blame for this—our stubborn insistence on avoiding ads. That's prompted marketers to attempt end runs around DVRs and our fast forwarding through their messages. Branded entertainment or product placement or integrations is their response to the sound of many hands zapping in an ever-more-fragmented and cluttered media landscape.

And how responsive they have been! DHL adapted "Accepting Impossible Missions Daily" as its tag line for being the official shipping and logistics partner of *Mission: Impossible III*. The Weinstein Brothers forged a multiyear marketing alliance with L'Oréal to integrate their cosmetics in their movies, even digitally inserting them after production. It didn't take two hours to decode Sony's plan in *The Da Vinci Code*: It was to push products even if it meant tinkering with Dan Brown's novel. In Brown's version, the villainous academic studies Leonardo da Vinci's works on the pages of a book; in the movie he does it on a Sony plasma screen.

In *Brokeback Mountain*, Ford pickups are more openly displayed than the movie's romance. They show up eight times. GMCs are seen seven times; Camel cigarettes, twice; and Budweiser, 13 times. A huge Coke sign appears behind Ennis's former girlfriend and an equally prominent one of Pepsi appears in the red-light district of the seedy Mexican town where Jack picks up a one-night stand. Ray-Ban sunglasses also occupied prime real estate (the stars' faces) in *Risky Business* and *Men in Black*. And in *Capote*, the author lavishes as much attention on bottles of J&B as he does on the killers he's writing about.

Tobacco companies have sashayed around their self-imposed prohibition of advertising on TV by getting into the *main frame*. The stars in almost every film nominated for an Oscar in 2006 smoked. *Brokeback Mountain, Capote, Good Night, and Good Luck*, and *Walk the Line* each included more than 50 scenes where key characters puff away.

By shouldering a share of the cost, marketers have become a critical component in movie-making. At least 30 Hollywood agencies have employees who do nothing but track circulated scripts to see how they can get products into them. (At many companies there's a person who makes sure the shows treat their brands well.) At Carat, the Carat Entertainment company develops integration ideas and funding to take to networks and studios. There's even an eBay-like web site, "Embed," providing buyers and sellers a marketplace for deals.

Television employs the same "invasion and assimilation" strategy to have brands mentioned in dialogue and appear in scenes, or have plots revolve around them. The design team on *Extreme Makeover: Home Edition* once created a Mustang-themed room for a deserving family, and hip-hopper Funkmaster Flex touted a Ford Excursion limousine and a Mustang GT convertible as what to drive to the prom on MTV's *Total Request Live*.

Marathon Ventures boasts that it can "tune out the effects of TiVo" by digitally "injecting" products into syndicated reruns of old TV shows. It has injected a box of Cheez-It brand crackers into CBS's sitcom *Still Standing*, and Ziploc bags into its *Out of Practice*. At the turn of the century (the 21st, that is), most TV product placement deals were bartered with advertisers' goods used as props. Now, in addition to footing part of the production bill, most advertisers also buy ads on the show into which they're integrating and on others in the network's inventory as well, and occasionally refer to those shows in their ads. It's no longer uncommon for an advertiser to pay the same cost per second to have a major placement in a show as it would have for a 30-second commercial adjacent to it.

On *Lost*, the group of plane-crash survivors cannot force their way into a silver attaché case made by Zero Halliburton. (Only the key to the case finally reveals its contents.) In an episode of *Sex and the City*, a salesgirl talks Miranda out of buying a diet book to sign up for Weight Watchers instead. *Friends* centered a show on a character's obsession with Pottery Barn. And when our hero, agent Jack Bauer, found himself away from his Expedition (remember his car of choice?) and stuck in an airport crawl space unable to rescue terrorized hostages, he used a Sprint Treo 650 to send headquarters photos of the hostages "clear enough for you to identify them."

Placements and their price tags vary across the lot. Research firm ITVX found the 3.5-minute inclusion of Outback Steakhouse in the May 8, 2006 episode of *The Apprentice*, where teams competed to sell the most Outback fare at a Rutgers–Navy tailgate party, was a coup with Donald Trump branding Outback a "great" restaurant and contestants gushing about its specialties. Another priceless product placement was scored by online dating service Perfectmatch.com. In the first episode of Lifetime's *Lovespring International* comedy, the owner of a dysfunctional dating service in California rages about the torrent of people who've signed up for Perfectmatch.com in the last five minutes. Perfectmatch is Lovespring's perpetual nemesis, stealing clients as a distinct part of the story. In one episode, an irritated client sneers, "I would have had better luck on Perfectmatch.com."

In 2005, Nielsen counted a whopping 7,514 placements on ESPN's *The Contender*, a competition for the next boxing superstar. That figure is almost double *American Idol*, its nearest rival, in total occurrences, but bouts ahead on a per-episode basis. Its 15 telecasts averaged 500.9 "product occurrences" placed in its shows, compared with a mere 83.3 per show of *Idol*. (The triumvirate of judges sits behind large Coca-Cola cups, and fans are reminded that they can text vote on their AT&T wireless.) Third-placed *Extreme Makeover: Home Edition*, with a total of 3,318 occurrences or 45.5 per episode, seemed like a lightweight in comparison. But size isn't everything. Even one product and a few hundred people in a darkened room are enough for a solid pitch.

Theater sponsorship used to mean a corporate name on a theater, signage in a lobby, and ads in the program. Even though the audience is small (figure 200 people) and the unions testy, marketers like that the audience is captive. Corporate sponsorship has crept onto the stage. A 2006 *New York Times* editorial whined that our lives are "already lived at the bottom of the slippery slope, buried in the debris of advertising"; how nice it would be to go to the theater "to be entertained and moved and not sold a bill of goods."

That was even before England's curtain call. In New York, the London Tourist Board presented the "world's first live theatrical commercial" at the start of *Stomp*. (It was also performed in a few other cities around the country as a prelude to different plays.) The lights dimmed and the pre-show silence was shattered by a cell phone. A theatergoer takes the call and starts yammering about visiting London to see her daughter as well as The Mattress Factory and the Tate Modern. The daughter is revealed on stage, sitting at her computer. Then the scene shifts to a young American at a London spa, talking by phone with her new British husband, discussing what they might do that night.

The New York Times may have been in a dither about product placement, but not everyone is vexed by it. Decima Research surveyed *CSI: Miami* fans and found that while 56 percent knew David Caruso drove a Hummer in the show, just 48 percent considered it intrusive. Sixty-nine percent even described it as effective marketing.

Only five years ago, product placers skulked about, sensing that what they were doing was wrong and reviled. It turns out only a very small segment of people are against it, says Dean Ayers, president of the Entertainment Resource and Marketing Association. (That's right, product placement even has its own trade organization and it's measured by Nielsen and by ITVX, which assigns a value based on the nature of the placement, such as whether the star touches the product—a "hero placement"—or if it's in the background. Now you know why the Coke sign was behind Ennis's girlfriend and why the men in black wore Ray-Bans.)

What's more, seeing the product in the story or hearing it mentioned seems to make people more receptive to its ads. As an experiment, Court TV produced three versions of a scene, ostensibly for its *Parco P.I.* show, integrating Reckitt Benckiser's Easy-Off BAM with varying degrees of intrusiveness and showed them to research participants. One version had a bottle of BAM in the kitchen; another had an investigator inform a family that they could use BAM to clean up a mess made by fingerprinting dust. The third showed the cleaning product being used while an investigator talked up its efficacy.

The three versions were shown with and without a traditional commercial for the product accompanying it. When the product placement flew solo (without a BAM commercial), 10 percent of viewers recalled its most subtle inclusion, 54 percent remembered when it was mentioned, and 56 percent when it was used. By itself, the commercial generated 62 percent recall, which edged up to 68 percent with the visual product placement, to 86 percent with a mention, but to only 84 percent when the product was used. Even more than recall, the products seemed to inspire goodwill, with much higher percentages of viewers very interested in using BAM after being subjected to the double barrel. Other studies show that roughly half of viewers notice brands placed in movies and on TV, and more than 60 percent claim to be willing to try them.

Although the Federal Trade Commission rejected the consumer advocacy group Commercial Alert's plea that programs disclose all product placement marketing arrangements on these shores, the European Union has been more of a stickler. Factions want to tighten rules so that no program partly funded by advertisers can be shown either on TV or in the cinema there. A 1995 directive allows product placements in films first shown in cinemas, but requires TV shows to obey the "separation principle" that essentially outlaws them. Yet there has been some movement to accept them in comedy and light entertainment, though definitely not in children's programming. Many placed products have surfaced on TV there anyway, either as imports from the United States, or planted there as a free prop legally—a kind of corporate mise-en-scene. Hence, in BBC's sitcom *Hardware*, set in a DIY store, the tool-making company, Stanley, is obvious.

Book publishers have also been seduced by marketers come courting. In 2001, Bulgari paid Fay Weldon to feature its Italian jewelry prominently in her novel, *The Bulgari Connection*. More recently, in the young-adult novel, *Cathy's Book: If Found Call (650) 266-8233*, the spunky heroine wears a "killer coat of Lipslicks." In *Daring*, Cover Girl teamed with Running Press to have its lip gloss showcased here in exchange for their promoting the book on Beinggirl.com, a web site for adolescent girls. When author Karin Slaughter put her protagonist behind the wheel of a BMW in her crime novels, the automaker tapped her publisher to produce short audio books with BMW cars in their plots. (Slaughter got to write one.) In one of the 35- to 60-minute stories (timed for the length of typical commutes), the wife of a California real estate investor accuses him of loving his car more than he loves her. "It's not a car," he snaps, "it's a BMW Z4."

The products of us mere mortals have even cozied up to superheroes in comic books. In DC Comics' new "Rush City," the hero drives a Pontiac Solstice. (No word on whether he ordered it after seeing the segment on *The Apprentice*.) Marvel inked Nike's "swoosh" into scenes of "New X-Men," and Dodge's Caliber is well-protected, popping up in "Spider-Man," "Captain America," and "Sub-Mariner". And for the younger crowd, it's hard to find a pee-wee counting book that's not a product plug. Skittles, Cheerios, Reese's Pieces, M&Ms, and Crayola crayons all have counting books. Twizzlers prefers to teach percentages, and Hershey's milk chocolate, fractions.

It might seem like the intersection of Madison and Vine is a new destination for marketers, but as far back as the 1930s, Procter & Gamble wove its soap powders into the stories on the radio and created "soap operas." (Even earlier, in 1908, "Take Me Out to the Ball Game" could be heard as an exhortation to buy Cracker Jack.) Advertisers' brands, product names, and logos were embroidered into such game, quiz, and talent shows as *The $64,000 Question, Beat the Clock, Arthur Godfrey's Talent Scouts,* and *Twenty-One.* At the same time, De Beers distributed sample diamonds to studios to use in roles that showed women being swayed by this coveted gift. Leading actors often smoked in movies and TV shows because cigarette companies subsidized "the glamour." In the opening credits of early episodes of *Bewitched,* the characters rode atop the Chevrolet logo.

It was cleverly handled in the last film the Marx Brothers ever made, *Love Happy,* in 1949. Harpo seems to be chased by billboards atop a roof, and ultimately escapes upon the flying red horse that is still Mobil's logo. Not long after that caper, Gordon's Gin actually paid to have Katharine Hepburn's character in the movie *The African Queen* hurl its booze overboard.

The most famous product placement plot twist involves *E.T., the Extra-Terrestrial.* In 1982, its producers approached M&Ms to have a close encounter with its candy, but Mars, fearful of the way they would be portrayed, turned them down. Reese's Pieces got the job, propelling the peanut-butter morsels into 65 percent more Halloween baskets.

Other marketers have gotten cold feet and insisted that their names be changed to escape criticism or maltreatment. That's how Nokia became Nokio on *Melrose Place.* Sometimes they don't even get the chance to say no. SC Johnson was caught off guard when its ant-killer Raid was hurled in a violent fight scene in *The Sopranos.* No one had sought its okay (and if they had, they'd have been refused).

Interest in product placement lulled and then revived in 1999, with the success of the prime-time quiz show *Who Wants to Be a Millionaire.* In an icon-eat-icon world, marketers like AT&T rushed to ABC to sponsor such features as the program's "phone-a-friend" ploy. Many appropriated the *Millionaire* catch phrase "Is that your final answer?" for their ad campaigns.

When Ken Jennings missed winning his 75th consecutive game by answering "FedEx" instead of "H&R Block," the delivery service ran an ad commending his record-breaking streak and noted, "There's only one time FedEx has ever been the wrong answer."

Now, it seems as if we've come full circle, with marketers making the showcase for their products instead of just buying time on them. Goen Group, which makes the diet pill Trimspa, developed the weight-loss reality show *Million Dollar Makeover Challenge*. Unilever built two specials around its Axe Shower body wash: "The Gamekillers" on MTV and "Exposing the Order of the Serpentine" on Spike TV. Both depicted the tribulations of lusty women-chasers. Mountain Dew financed *First Descent*, a documentary on snowboarding in which it made appearances, and Procter & Gamble sponsored episodes of the Nick at Nite sitcom, *At the Poocharellis*,' in which its Febreze fabric care product is woven into the plot.

Some call the rash of product plugs in shows invasive and complain that it's turning prime-time into infomercialville. Others worry that if they're not doing it already, sponsors *will* dictate how their show plays. (Greyhound, for example, demanded that a scene from *The Simple Life: Interns* that portrayed a skidding bus for a laugh be pulled.)

Show writers fret that the ubiquity of product placements in television shows will wash away already-declining audiences. But most advertisers realize that they have to be subtle so as not to offend viewers—but prominent enough to be noticed.

13

DATA MINING: WHY YOUR TV MAY THINK YOU'RE GAY

I f you're a TiVo guy who watched *Angels in America* and who, on occasion, has kicked back for *Queer Eye for the Straight Guy* and *Will and Grace*, television has got your number. If you've no clue what an exfoliant is, it's probably the wrong number, but chances are this machine that's become your pal will recommend you look at *Boy Meets Boy* on Bravo, *Queer as Folk* on Showtime, perhaps some Martha Stewart, and a smattering from Lifetime, known jokingly as "The Network for Women . . .and gay men."

Some straight guys who've found themselves mistakenly outed by TiVo have resorted to counterprogramming ploys. They've parked the TV at the wrestling channel and pretended to be captivated by *Fantasy Football* so as to "reset" their all-knowing TV search engine/guide.

TiVo, a former Carat client, is constantly in motion and hard to fool. It scours the TV listings for the upcoming two weeks, alert for the shows or keyword search strings that you've entered in the past. Then based on your prior choices, this oh-so-efficient butler will convert its search results into suggestions for your viewing pleasure.

TiVo is just one manifestation of where marketing is migrating: to hear you (in and) out and offer what they think you'd like, based on what they've heard. It's the next stage of data mining and it's been done in rudimentary form long before Amazon.com recommended Zadie Smith's *On Beauty* to readers who savored Ian McEwan's *Saturday* because other Amazon customers with what they've identified as similar tastes endorsed it.

Analytics and ROI calculations are the hottest area in marketing today. Everybody wants to know what's working and what is not. The media research people and the insight groups of the big media services companies have become the new rock stars of their organizations. Companies like Marketing Management Analytics (MMA), which pioneered the use of multivariate regression analysis to calculate ROI, have created real-time analytics so brand managers can monitor all customers, sales, and marketing activity in real time. This Bloomberg of marketing watches for aberrations in volume at call centers, in ongoing awareness-tracking data, or in supermarket scanner sales numbers, and calculate ROI constantly. Proprietary tools like Carat's FORTEL show in real time what commercials are stickiest and where, and what works best against certain audiences and has them leaning forward in their seats.

Now, rather than merely respond to data (the college suspends a drug user who posts his illegal exploits on a web site), companies are calling on these tools to predict behavior—determining, for example, what brand of vodka a married woman with three children is most likely to buy. (Indeed, Google began predicting the future when it offered ads tied to users' search. In their datasphere, your typing in "dog breeders" or "digital cameras" signaled your intentions to share your home with both.)

Privacy defenders have raised a ruckus over the government poking its nose into our lives in the form of electronic eavesdropping (specifically the National Security Agency and the database of two trillion telephone calls it has amassed to hunt al-Qaeda operatives). But the truth is that Americans willingly give away a great deal more information about themselves than even the most astute Sherlock Holmes could tease out. Fueled by the desire for discounts, to be entertained, to belong to a group, to communicate on the fly, to have our wishes instantly gratified, to get information instantly and for free, you've opened the door wide for marketers to watch what you do and then catalog it and you.

Ever wonder how your ATM screen knows to greet you by name, or how, when you call your newspaper to arrange for a vacation stop in delivery, they know where you live before you tell them? Have you got your phone number listed . . . or better yet, ever make a call? Every phone call (and text message) from your landline and mobile is documented somewhere. Have you got GPS technology in your car? That's a two-way homing device. Do you subscribe to magazines? They sell your name, addresses, and any other goods they have on you. If you buy stuff online, use your credit card at the gas pump, or rent a movie, the personal information related to these transactions is stored in thousands of public and private databases. In fact, it's said that the average American appears in some 50 commercial databases. Google alone stores every search query that's ever been typed on its engine.

What all this means is that people who mine those databases can easily learn where and how much ice cream you bought—and what brand and flavor. They know what music you like, what books you've borrowed, when you've gained a few extra pounds and can't fit into your old clothes, and what countries you've visited. They know when you had your last oil change, how much cash you carry and when you usually visit the ATM, and even how much you paid for your house and how much it's worth now. They also know if you've ever made an insurance claim against it. And they know all this because you've invited them to know it. (Have you ever read the privacy policy or user agreement on the back of any of your contracts? It's the equivalent of ski at your own risk.)

This isn't science fiction circa 2026. It's computer science fact circa 2006. Many people reflexively shudder that Big Business/Big Brother is some insidious force out to harm them. We think TiVo addicts (even those miscategorized) know better. They *love* their butler. Believe it or not, marketers mine data to sell you better and more efficiently, to serve up what you're interested in, like Polygrip to the toothless. Why waste money advertising on the CBS news if more than 9 out of 10 viewers there have teeth? You could liken this analysis of customer information to a return to the intimacy of a small-town general store where the pro-prietor knew who favored molasses cookies and who liked anise licorice.

Back in the olden days of 2000, gathering data from multiple sources and compiling it into easily understandable and useful reports was a mammoth task. Now, with improvements in hardware, software, and the Net, it's routine, and routinely deployed. Artur Dubrawski, director of the data-mining Auton Lab at Carnegie Mellon University, says corporate data collection—and "data aggregators" who collect information from many sources, repackage it, and then sell it—has rocketed. Their software can sort through massive databases and connect the dots to spot patterns instantly, a task that would take humans years to do, if they could do it at all.

There's an oft-repeated tale of how 7-Eleven, which analyzes information on millions of transactions a day, correlated sales of diapers with beer after theorizing and then confirming that young dads popped in on their way home from work to pick up the former, and impulsively added the latter to their shopping baskets. The omnipresent retailer stocked the two items side by side on its shelves, and sales rocketed.

That's a tall tale, a mythical illustration of data mining's possibilities. A real one comes from British chain Tesco, a pioneer in data mining applications. (Tesco has 31.5% of the market share in food in the U.K.) Thirteen million Britons have traded personal information for their Tesco Clubcards, which earn them discounts and tailored offers.

Brits, data, and food seem to go together. Another U.K. supermarket was about to discontinue a line of pricey French cheeses that were not moving briskly. But data mining showed that the few people who were buying those cheeses were among the store's most profitable customers. The store opted to keep the fromage so as to keep those customers. Pubs in England also use real-time data mining to change the prices of drinks daily based on the impact that "happy hour" has on sales. If discounting an ale, say, boosts sales one day, they keep that discount. If not, it's on to another brand in search of the brass ring.

Harrah's Entertainment keeps profiles of millions of its customers including their ages, gender, and zip codes, as well as how long they spent gambling and how much they won or lost. With this they can target individuals with offers, from getaway weekends to gourmet dining, designed to get the greatest returns. MovieTickets.com is focused on learning how consumers pick movies. The fledgling Colorado company, Umbria, which sifts through millions of blogs in real time, recently found that guys look to Gatorade to ease hangovers and that bawdy Burger King online ads alienate lots of people—but not the young guys who are its prime customer. They lap it up.

The hub of Uncle Sam's "dataveillance" is an R&D program within the Department of Homeland Security called ADVISE (Analysis, Dissemination, Visualization, Insight, and Semantic Enhancement). Yet governments mine data to capture more than terrorists. Slicing and dicing data, the Pentagon deduces which branch of the military will most appeal to a prospective recruit. Do you expect to marry in the next year? Maybe you're a Navy man. If you read *Bassmaster* magazine, check out the Air Force. Do you listen to Spanish radio? The Army's gotcha. Read *Car Craft* and *Outdoor Life*? You're on the Marines' radar screen.

For years, the Texas Comptroller's Office suspected that wealthy residents were purchasing private planes out of state to avoid sales taxes. In the six months after the office installed new data mining and warehousing technology that matched federal airplane registrations with state tax records, the lone star state collected $5 million in unpaid taxes from 43 scofflaws. Massachusetts, Iowa, Virginia, and California have similar systems: In one year the latter collected an extra $184 million in unpaid taxes from 600,000 nonfilers. And, of course, politicians rely on mined data to frame their campaign messages.

Long before companies began collecting and aggregating information and combining it with outside data, supermarkets used bar codes and customer-loyalty cards to find out what sold and to whom. To get the card, a customer filled out an application that amounted to a purchase profile. Essentially, shoppers traded a window on their carts for special offers and cents off on their purchases. Use of the card also helped grocers with inventory control and product placement. Loyalty cards are almost ubiquitous now—in bookstores, drugstores, and gas stations. CVS says more than 50 million of its ExtraCare cards are in use, and two-thirds of its sales are made with them.

Many programs are run behind the scenes by Catalina Marketing, which collects loyalty and bulk sales data from more than 20,000 stores, then uses it to create pictures of shoppers over time so it can ultimately suggest to a regular purchaser of Alpo that she switch to Iams dog food, with a discount incentive, of course. Many of these offers will be delivered to that wireless technology piece in your pocket as you cruise the grocer's aisles. Indeed, at some point, you may never again need to write another shopping list.

Beyond loyalty cards, supermarkets run data-mining software of sales receipts on certain items to determine if, say, the shrimp cocktail sauce sold better when displayed at the fish counter. And radio frequency identification tags or tiny computer chips are replacing bar codes, eventually allowing retailers to track products long after they've left the store.

How the cookie crumbles is a bit different online, but the behavioral targeting mission is the same. Visit a web retailer or portal such as Yahoo!'s free search and they plant a small data file or cookie on your computer that tracks where you go every time you visit the site. Sign on and many sites will greet you with a reminder of what you've browsed there on prior visits. And if you've searched for electric grass trimmers, you just might find an ad for Stiehl or Echo's machines winking at you the next time you sign on. Microsoft, which has collected the name, age, gender, and Zip code of everyone using its free Hotmail e-mail, combines it with other data, like when the Hotmailer usually signs on to serve marketers (and themselves, of course). It can sell an ad at a premium from a local florist to deliver a coupon during lunch hour on Valentine's Day to 30-to-40-year-old men making good money.

Statisticians have long used regression models and standard deviation to make actuarial tables and body mass standards, say. Predictive analytics goes way beyond that to anticipate what you'll buy (so a store will have enough in stock) and who will be the better candidate for the job (so the company will hire her). It also lets companies create what-if scenarios so they can access their options with something akin to insider information. Using what-if modeling, the Absa Group of South Africa slashed the number of armed robberies at its bank, even while the incidences rocketed throughout the country overall, and Banco Espírito Santo kept large numbers of customers who were on their way out the door from defecting. By mining county land records, Zillow.com speculates on the value of 67 million U.S. homes. By mining the global positioning satellite receivers of commercial vehicles and factoring in weather conditions and special events scheduled, Inrix predicts traffic patterns in 15 cities.

What-if modeling lets retailers cluster their customers by persona, like dinks (dual income no kids), for example. It lets marketers abandon a commoditized, 30-second ad world for one that sells communities: "Hey, Chevy dealer, here's a whole bunch of Honda drivers—what do you want to tell them?"

Working for Talbots, for example, a Carat company, Molecular, determined that four out of five of its customers who go online would not buy through the web site. For one thing, they felt they needed to try on the clothes they were considering buying. For another, they felt no need to pay shipping charges when Talbots stores are everywhere. And because many customers were traditional middle-aged women, they felt timid about putting credit card information out there. Armed with this intelligence, Molecular recommended making the web site less transactional and more personal and accommodating. Customers could preview clothes and have what they wanted to try on, in their size and color, assembled and waiting for them in the dressing room at a set time. Talbots' smart personal-shoppers would have added their own suggestions of clothes or accessories that went well with the shopper's picks. Sales per customer soared.

Goaded by watchdog groups such as the Center for Digital Democracy, which predicts that ultimately data mining will be used to manipulate us into determining whom we should pray to and vote for, companies have vowed not to sell their data or identify individuals from it. (Catalina, for instance, uses only ID numbers and other anonymization techniques by converting names and Social Security numbers into a meaningless jumble of letters and digits that lets data-mining software search and correlate separate databases—without decrypting individuals.) Microsoft has promised not to buy an individual's income history—just the average income from his or her Zip code. Publix abandoned its data-mining efforts because of privacy concerns. In 2000, after DoubleClick ignited a public uproar and Congressional hearings when it announced that it would cross-reference anonymous web-surfing data with personal data collected by an offline data broker on the subject, it jettisoned the plan.

It is not likely that too many companies will be jettisoning these plans any more, though, because to do so would risk falling behind their rivals on many fronts. This tipping point has come and gone; this (cash) cow is out of the barn.

We don't think it's a bad thing. Searching for products (by price, availability, quality, and any other variable) will become a whole lot easier. Consumers will be able to maximize how much they can get for their home or car within one week or within two months. They'll be able to pick a surgeon to deal with the stenosis in their backs based on data-mined results. They'll even know if they should spring for that airline seat now, or wait until tomorrow.

The latter is courtesy of Oren Etzioni, a computer science professor at the University of Washington, who was so ticked off when he discovered that he'd paid more for a flight than his seatmate, who'd even booked later, that he invented Farecast, which predicts how much the price of an airline ticket will rise or fall over the coming days. Etzioni, who'd originally named the search engine Hamlet as a play on the "To buy or not to buy" motto, mines information about seat supply and demand and applies an algorithm to predict how the airlines will use so-called dynamic pricing, at a moment's notice, dropping a fare to fill up an otherwise-empty seat or hiking the seat cost for a flight predicted to be packed.

You'd be hard-pressed to find a TiVo owner who isn't pleased with the way his mind is read, or an ad person pleased by the prospect of TiVo. In fact, both should be pleased. TiVo is not the enemy of the ad industry. It's a catalyst and accelerant. By letting consumers do what they want, it's forcing marketers to engage them, to give them what they both want—a customer who wants to be sold.

14

SEARCH: HOW AUBUCHON BESTED THE HARDWARE GOLIATHS

The Aubuchon family émigrés into the United States from Canada in 1901 opened their first hardware store in Fitchburg, Massachusetts, in February 1908. By 1930 there were eight stores in central Massachusetts, and by 1948, 32 in the Northeast. Today the company operates 135 neighborhood hardware stores throughout New England, and pops up fourth from the top when you type in "hardware store" on a Google search.

How did this mom-and-pop Aubuchon outfit manage to beat out Sears Roebuck, in fifth place in the listings, and land three spots ahead of Lowe's?

It gamed search. Tweaking its site via search engine optimization, Aubuchon (or more accurately the media brains behind it) got natural (vs. paid-for) results high on search return pages. That's a critical marketing maneuver as 62 percent of searchers don't go past the first page and 9 out of 10 never make it beyond the third page. Not playing to the algorithms is like putting up a billboard in the woods.

It's not just that the company's web site would be on an untrafficked backwater; it's that its absence from the winning team brands it a loser.

Thirty-six percent of all search engine users believe companies whose web sites are listed organically on the first page are the top brands and the best ones. Browsers "convert" to buyers from organic search at three times the rate of those of paid search.

The banner and button are dead, but online search could not be more robust. In the time it takes three new babies to enter the world and 544 McDonald's customers to be served (one second), some 2,315 Google searches will have been initiated—nearly twice the number of ATM transactions (1,268). By the time you finish this page, 200,000 would-be car buyers and 5,000 would-be brides will have researched wheels and weddings respectively. Even if they know a web site address, most people get to Delta via a search engine rather than typing the airline's URL into the address bar. Indeed, using search to navigate the Net is so ordinary that *google* has become an accepted verb.

Not surprisingly, where people congregate, marketers penetrate. Beyond their mere presence, searchers offer something even more delectable. They are prospects who have initiated the contact. They're looking to be sold.

Marketers have three ways to sell them here: pay-per-click ads, paid inclusion listings, and organic search results in the unpaid search engine results pages. In 2006, marketers spent more than $7 billion on paid search, up from $5.1 billion in 2005. They're expected to spend $11 billion by 2009 on these text ads adjacent to organic results from online searches; marketers buy the rights for their ads to appear on-screen when computer users type in key words. Piper Jaffray says that globally the paid search industry will top $33 billion in 2010.

With pay-per-click ads, advertisers pay only when their ad is clicked on, but fraudsters have abused the pay-per-click model to saddle their rivals with bills for phantom customers. Then too, 7 out of 10 people viewing search results choose the organic listings first. And the price per click on the average paid search has rocketed from $0.35 in 2003 to almost $2 now. Between September 2005 and December 2005 alone, according to DoubleClick, the average cost per keyword increased from $22.50 to $54.62, a 114 percent surge. Internet stalwarts like FTD, eBay, and Blue Nile have whined about the absurd escalation of keyword prices. On top of all this, the number of keywords marketers use in paid search campaigns has mushroomed. General Motors, for example, is said to be in the market for more than one million keywords. Today, the average paid search advertising campaign targets more than 1,000 keyword phrases.

Demand can propel the cost of adjacencies to certain even arcane search words. Mesothelioma, a lung cancer caused by exposure to asbestos, was driven to more than $50 per click by law firms eager for a share of lucrative asbestos-related settlements. Online auctions for words take place many times a day with the bid prices of many keywords fluctuating constantly, spiking at certain times of the day or days of the week, and even in certain months (preceding Christmas, for instance). Automated bidding agents, once a luxury, are becoming commonplace, raising and lowering bids on tens of thousands of keywords at once, based on how well those keywords performed historically at that hour of the day, and day of the week. These bid agents also optimize to specific return-on-investment levels. For example, if a buyer instructs the system to pay no more than $5 for every sale made, the bid agent will keep the cost per click at a level where that $5 CPA (cost per action, or cost per acquisition) is possible. These tools make the bid landscape more dynamic than ever before and help advertisers achieve measurable, predictable goals.

Some companies are in the market for creative approaches to avoid buying the priciest ads, link words like "automotive" or "Oscars," say, which would redirect searchers to sponsored sites. Some have gone into vertical versus horizontal search. Type "ceramics" into Google and a swarm of pottery sites appears. Type it into Dentalproducts.net and take your pick of reinforced and restored dental cosmetics. Vertical search engines allow users to find very specific search results on very specific topics, so marketers in those topic areas can find targeted audiences relatively cheaply.

In other cases, marketers have used side doors to find inexpensive keywords. Type "mustache" into Google and up comes the mustachioed chairman of Chrysler, prominent from Daimler's ads. Seventy-year-old Muzak has added misspellings of its brand name.

When Honda launched its Element truck it invited audiences to interact with a talking crab, possum, and lizard and bought cheaper keywords you wouldn't connect with a car. Bidding for "possum," it was up against pest control peddlers and sellers of possum T-shirts.

Its keywords were cheaper than "car" but certainly not cheap, which is why more and more marketers are spending big on organic search engine optimization. They can do it the white-hat way or the black-hat way, no kidding. White-hat methods are accepted (if not endorsed) by search engines. Google engineer Matt Cutts blogs on how sites can make themselves more visible to automated software spiders.

White-hat techniques include building content and improving site quality and a host of technical tactics like separating the Javascript (the code that enables clever effects like pop-ups) and CSS (the code that contains styling information, such as typefaces, colors, and sizes of text) files from the HTML (the base code for all web pages) files to make the site more user and search engine friendly. White-hat SEOs attempt to discover and correct mistakes, such as machine-unreadable menus, broken links, temporary redirects, or a poor navigation structure.

Dynamic, updated web sites with fresh, original content also attract search engines, as do including accurate image tags (the text that pops up to describes each web site image when a cursor runs over it) and differentiating web sites with descriptive language: Forget "a great, friendly hotel" and go with "four-star luxury hotel in Atlanta." People search the way they talk, using either "sofa" or "couch," for example, or "soda" or "pop." Descriptions should match phrases they use to search. An online store in Thailand selling Kaw Kwy statues saw sales soar after it substituted the search term "Fake Ivory."

Nefarious black-hat techniques are usually unrelated to providing quality content to web site users and are entirely related to attracting clicks at any cost. With spamdexing and cloaking (spamming the Web with dummy pages full of links to make their sites appear popular, and serving one version of a page to search engine spiders/bots and another version to human visitors respectively) blackhatters promote irrelevant (primarily) commercial pages by abusing search engine algorithms.

The search engines, of course, retaliate for being trifled with. They reduce the rankings of the blackhatters or eliminate their listings from search page results altogether. In February 2006, Google removed BMW Germany for "cyberstealth marketing" by embedding invisible keywords into their sites to ensure they come out at the top of Google listings. *The Wall Street Journal* reported how Google banished Traffic Power for using hidden text without informing its clients.

So much a part of the search engine culture are these shady, unethical techniques that the blackhatseo.com web site parodies such skullduggery exposés as Google Bowling—trying to knock out competitors that rank above you in Google search results by making those rivals' sites look bad to Google.

While search engine optimizers study every Google, Yahoo!, and Microsoft patent application and search-algorithm upgrade to figure out how to play it, most search engines keep their methods and ranking algorithms well-guarded secrets, so as to collect the best search results and outfox spammers in this ongoing game of one-upmanship. Whenever Google updates its algorithm and the organic results are reranked, it is known as the Google Dance. Google understands this well (they even have an event on their campus in Mountain View, California, once a year for search engine marketing experts, aptly called "the Google Dance"), but remains mum on its exact techniques. Search engines can employ dozens if not hundreds of factors in ranking the listings on their search results pages, and those factors change constantly. They also differ from one search engine to the next: A web page that ranks number 1 on ASK.com could be number 150 on Yahoo!.

E-Loan's SEO team calculates the ROI for each one of its 250,000 key words and phrases that whisk its ad next to the left-hand findings on your screen results. And it tweaks thousands of bids by the hour, making minuscule changes to the ad text to see if it squeezes out a dollop more juice. Yet almost 40 percent of marketers don't calculate their return on investment in search, and one in three doesn't track conversion rates. That means they're bidding for placement without knowing if their ads pay for themselves. And many who attempt the calculations don't account for the fact that more than three out of four purchases following an online search are made offline as people abandon clicks for brick-and-mortar. But few marketers connect these dots. Nor do many anticipate the spike in search referrals that comes on the heels of new TV, radio, or print commercials or a direct mail campaign. Search bleeds into every other channel, and everything in advertising impacts search. At the cash register of the future, instead of asking for your Zip code, the clerk will ask if you'd gone online before coming in.

And search is expanding beyond the Internet. GPS in the car is search in your auto. You'll also see more search-to-phone follow-up where web surfers can click to talk live to an advertiser's salesperson. The giant online auction site eBay recently bought Skype, enabling its customers to make free computer-to-computer phone calls. (Actually, the advertiser pays eBay but doesn't mind as faking calls is harder than faking clicks.) And now Google and eBay have teamed up to enable Google advertisers to benefit from the popularity and functionality of Skype, signaling a bet from the industry that more and more consumers will find what they're looking for on a search engine but want to have a phone conversation before completing the transaction.

It's also recasting journalism. The inverted-pyramid structure of a news article, taught in journalism schools for decades (shaped by the telegraph, the Internet of its day, which mandated making the most significant points first), will give way to headlines and opening paragraphs laced with highly linked words. These newscasts will play to search engines whose relevance factor hinges on the proximity of one word to another (words that are next to or near one another in an article are deemed related by search engines) and that attempt to weed out errant meanings that a totally literal engine might not recognize. A search for a "driver," for example, might yield a communications device for a computer, a golf club, a person in a car, or something that turns a screw.

There will also be more transparency in search and more intelligent algorithms that are predictive, semantic, linguistic, and heuristic. Search engines will get to know a user's searching habits and try to anticipate his or her interests, just as TiVo recommends TV shows based on previous viewings and Amazon suggests books to its customers based on their prior purchases. Search engines will become more specialized. Technorati.com, for example, specializes in finding blogs, and BrightPlanet charts some of the big business and government databases missed by Google et al. Even with over four billion web pages, Google has mapped perhaps only 1/500th of what's out there. Local searching will become a lot more important, too.

Search represents exactly where civilization is going. People are learning to get exactly what they want when they want it. Optimizing search may be the real definition of broadcasting—sowing seeds everywhere on the Web for consumers to click on.

15

Why Honda Hates the Internet . . . and Those Who Haunt It

In the dark ages of the early 1990s, before web sites such as Edmunds.com began publishing the invoice prices of cars for all to see, dealers maximized their profit by shrouding the deal. It wasn't an especially daunting task, as most new-car buys involved a welter of variables including trade-in value, interest rate, different loan terms, and a bevy of fees. In the old way of moving metal, salespeople practiced psychological tricks on "ups" (as customers who strolled into the showroom were called) to stoke their excitement for the car, and employed numerical legerdemain on the "four-square" worksheet they used to negotiate a typical car deal, starting with the sticker price and working down and angling to squeeze more from the back end, such as in higher finance charges.

Once the Internet pulled away the cloak, a car shopper could find the invoice price, add the requisite 2 to 3 percent profit, and make an offer, take-it-or-leave-it. Today, more than four out of five of Ford's U.S. customers have gone online before going into the showroom. Most come to the dealer with a spec sheet showing just what they want and what they're prepared to pay for it.

More than spurting gas prices it's the Internet that has stolen the joy (and profits) out of getting a prospect to "feel the wheel to seal the deal." Dealers have been coerced by competition into opening Internet departments, providing rock-bottom price quotes and competing with their on-floor sales crew, who won't even offer a quote until they feel the buyer is committed, for fear a casual looker will take a good price and shop it at another dealer.

Forget the MSRP (manufacturer's suggested retail price): The Net is disabling the very concept of fixed pricing by enabling people to find the same product at various prices from various vendors, and scour the universe for price discounts, coupons, and rebate offers.

Automotive dealers are hardly the only retailers hung out to dry by the Net and its revelations. Indeed, even as coupon inserts remain the second-most-read part of the Sunday newspaper, after the front page, many of the roughly 300 billion coupons distributed annually in the United States are migrating online, their sponsors trading inefficient shotgun paper coupons for the Internet's laser. While in 2005 online coupons still accounted for less than 1 percent of coupons out there, their use is growing by more than 50 percent a year. The two are not warring. Database web sites like coupon.mom.com are virtual organizers of coupon offers in newspaper circulars across the country. Web sites that collect offers from retailers (on everything from computers to cauliflower) and present them as one-stop shops for bargain seekers attracted some 166 million unique users in one month. About 15 percent of coupons printed online are redeemed compared to far less than 1 percent from Sunday newspapers, and merchants can change their offers in real time instead of dealing with printing and distribution in the offline world.

In 2006, online sales topped $210 billion, a 20 percent spike from the $176.4 billion the National Retail Federation's Shop.org reported in 2005, and nearly double what online sales were three years earlier. That is just the dollars moved by click. It doesn't begin to tell the story of the online channel's impact on sales offline and overall.

No matter whether they buy online or in store, 62 percent of shoppers go to the Web for information as part of their purchase decision process for all kinds of stuff. In 2006, at least three out of every four U.S.

mobile phone buyers researched on the Web, although just 5 percent actually bought there. They check out the phone's features, see what the service package covers, and find out what other users say about it.

It's not just the transparency of price quotes they find helpful, but the collaborative environment where others weigh in with alternative recommendations and their own experiences with the brand. Supposedly, one in four people has posted reviews of products or services online to help other shoppers. Jupiter Research reported that 48 percent of online shoppers find it critical that retailers post product reviews written by real people, which have become the most-used form of consumer-generated content on the Web. And a new phenomenon, the "coupon train," has emerged both offline and on, where people share coupons with each other.

In a 2006 study, the "Long and Winding Road: The Route to the Cash Register," Yahoo! identified four distinct purchasing paths people take. Packaged goods like toothpaste and barbecue sauce are often quick paths involving little consideration. Retail goods like waffle irons and body weights often take a winding route involving a modicum of comparison shopping between different channels. Technology, particularly when you're talking real money, involves a long path of researching various options over time; and big-ticket items like autos and annuities entail a consideration path that's both long and winding.

Yahoo! also found that the Internet has changed the shape of the traditional purchase funnel. Before, consumers, who on average considered three brands before picking one, steadily narrowed their choices enroute to purchase. During the traditional four stages of the "purchase tumbler" (researching a purchase, streamlining options, deciding where to buy, and making a final decision), consumers now turn to the Net (more even than to friends and family, offline reviews, and traditional media sources) and are open to new suggestions floated there. Rather than narrowing their choices, the Internet often broadens them.

Broadband has made the Web more of a sales tool with its ability to showcase products (beyond travel and credit-cards, with which it began) in creative ways such as 360-degree views, or recall details of previous purchases so as to guide current ones. In 2005, for the first time, more

Americans connected to the Web than to cable and more of them did so via broadband than dial-up. One result is more time spent online and a richer, more interactive experience. Another result is less interest in leaving home. In South Korea, where 75 percent of homes have broadband, fewer venture outside, hence fewer buy cars or attend sports games.

Broadband's widening penetration bodes well for the future of online shopping. For lots of reasons (avoiding shipping charges and waiting for delivery, fears of posting their credit/debit cards in cyberspace, the pleasure of touching merchandise and trying it on, etc.), people still prefer to spend money at brick-and-mortar locales. But rising gas prices could cut outings to stores and spur more online buying, which already has been growing at least three times as fast as retail sales overall. Travel remains the most popular product bought online, followed by computer hardware and software, and then autos and auto parts.

Stores have tried to mesh their online and physical-world personas. Some offer cybercoupons to use in their stores. Others let customers in the store order merchandise out of stock. J. C. Penney's jcp.com kiosks, available at all of its 35,000 checkout registers, let customers reserve a size or color of what they want in the store's next shipment. Other retailers have followed in Circuit City's and Best Buy's footprints, letting customers order online and guaranteeing that their pickup would await them at a local store.

And, of course, shoppers use their net-enabled phones at the store to compare prices. In Japan, where everyone has a web-enabled camera phone, people photograph bar codes off product packages and upload them to Amazon.co.jp. A quick tap into Amazon's online database reveals if the warehouse stocks it and what it costs and allows the online alternative to snatch away a sale on the spot. We're expecting that by 2010 digital cell phones with location-tracking and automatic short-range communication technology will be commonplace, and that electronic coupons will be delivered to these devices on demand and redeemed by whisking the phone past a cash register scanner (goodbye paper).

Inspired by the success of in-store personal shoppers getting customers to buy more, many retail web sites have ratcheted up the chatter.

Now, online chat specialists materialize whenever software determines that a slight nudge would turn a "maybe" into ka-ching.

When a visitor to Bluefly searches for more than three items in five minutes, a pop-up window opens with a friendly face offering help. And if a prospect stalls on the checkout page for more than one minute, the Bluefly service rep again steps forward. Lands' End interrupts the search of serious shoppers (those who've clicked on several items on its site) with a reminder that an online shopping assistant is standing by to help complete the order. Robert LoCascio, chief executive of LivePerson chat technology, says 1 in 10 customers who use a "click to chat" button on a product page go on to buy something.

That kind of black-and-white accounting is one reason why Internet advertising revenue has rocketed, and we expect it to continue orbiting. (In 2005 it topped $12.5 billion.) That's netting some surprising catches for the first medium able to provide advertisers with detailed information on how many viewers they're getting and how many are responding by clicking. In 2006, General Mills (Cheerios, Betty Crocker baking mixes) and Kraft (Jell-O, Kool-Aid) virtually doubled their online-ad spending and Unilever (Dove soap, Hellmann's mayonnaise) slashed its TV budget to move money online after cybertactics made Suave shampoo sales sparkle.

Banks have long known that once a customer pays even one bill online, there's an almost zero likelihood he'll transfer to another bank. Drug companies know they can pump up sales by e-reminding patients to take their meds and renew their prescriptions.

Every marketing dollar Pontiac had earmarked to introduce its sporty G5 coupe in late 2006 was spent online. The car maker's marketing director, Mark-Hans Richer, commented that this "radical experiment" wouldn't make the G5 as top of mind as a TV blitz but that Pontiac could reach its prime audience of young men for 60 to 70 percent less than a traditional $25 million to $30 million car launch.

Ironically, so many newcomers have tried to mine cybergold and pushed up the prices in this frontier that such Internet stalwarts as 1-800 Flowers and Netflix Inc. have moved chunks of their budgets offline! Indeed, Kraft spends around the same amount for holiday-time banner ads on major portals like MSN.com and Yahoo!'s main page that spring to life as recipes when a cursor crosses over them as they would to run a 30-second spot on *C.S.I.* So coveted is prime space on these heavily visited portals that an upfront similar to television's has emerged. And to land on this boardwalk, marketers are required to buy ad space in the portal's boonies.

Because marketers can monitor the meanderings of the mouse (ah, those cookies), many have figured out how to game the system. Some plant ads for HDTV screens, say, before someone who's demonstrated his interest by checking out related web sites, on other less expensive web-estate that he has visited, like where's the best snowboarding in Vermont.

Others, like Home Depot, want companies whose merchandise they carry to advertise on their web sites, presenting it as an opportunity to reach not a random set of eyeballs but someone who expressed interest in the merchandise on that page. Procter & Gamble bought Crest ads on the Wal-Mart web site promoting a dental-care bonus pack, and Unilever used the space to publicize in-store events for its Sunsilk hair line.

Airline web sites let fliers book tickets and seats, manage their travel awards and upgrades, print boarding passes—and buy stuff. ShopBlue from JetBlue, for example, has turned its web site into a virtual department store, selling (in addition to plane tickets and model airplanes) jewelry, clothing, cosmetics, travel posters, office supplies, bar accessories, and toys. United's Ted does a thriving business with people named Ted. For airlines, e-commerce means incremental revenue and a cheap way to market their product.

Mouse meanderings aren't all marketers monitor. Using sophisticated eye-tracking equipment, Nielsen Norman Group determined that people read web pages in an "F" pattern—longer sentences at the top of a page and less and less as they scroll down, making the first two words of a sentence critical. The Fremont, California, firm also found that web users connect well with images of attractive people looking directly at them, as long as the people are neither gorgeous nor suggestive of professional models (unapproachable).

Online shopping behavior is another area under the microscope. ComScore Networks found that men prefer sites brimming with product pictures, details, and specs, while women want to see the product in a lifestyle context. Its "Gender on the Net: Why It Matters, Where It's Missing, How It Should Work" report found that women are far more likely than men to enlarge a color swatch or rotate an item to view it from different angles, while men are more likely to dig deep to find discounts and the best deal and pick up their online purchase in the store.

Of course, online is about more than commerce. Since the TV networks began offering their hit shows as paid-for or ad-subsidized downloads, it's been about convergence with TV. Major portals like AOL, Yahoo!, and Microsoft are, or are becoming, channels. Legendary producer Mark Burnett, for example, created "Gold Rush," a real-life treasure-hunt program to air on AOL's web site with clues sprinkled throughout the AOL network. At the same time, it's about recognizing the uniqueness of both strands. Internet ads started out copying what's on TV, but that fizzled. Disney was among the first to recognize this and took to selling two sets of ads—TV commercials and online ads—for a single show. New ad forms for shows in streaming online video, where it is presumed viewers lean forward versus slouch back (i.e., they're more alert), are (or soon will be) the norm. There'll be less single-advertiser dominance and more interactivity, the hallmark of the Web 2.0 generation.

As for all those car dealers who hate the Net, they'll soon have another nemesis, or, opportunity, if you will. By 2010, most people will use VOD (video on demand) as their key research tool to shop a car. Instead of peering at a small screen, they'll actually choose to watch long-form ads or infomercials on a large screen. Call it the silver lining.

16

WHY GROWN MEN
VISIT LEGOLAND

I n 1968, in the center of Denmark's Jutland Peninsula, on what was
once a potato and dairy farm, the late Ole Kirk Christiansen, a car-
penter who founded Lego (and whose descendants still control it),
erected Legoland. The 25-acre amusement park, built from 42 million of its modular plastic bricks, was both an unwitting precursor to
Florida's Disney World and a pioneer in the hot arena of experiential marketing, where companies bring their brands into physical contact with
their customers as well as their prospective customers.

The toys, named Lego from *leg godt*, Danish for "play well" (which
also means "I study" and "I put together" in Latin), reflect the company's
philosophy of getting kids to turn on their imaginations and turn off the
TV. So do the theme park's thousands of waist-high re-creations of international landmarks configured from millions of thumbnail-size stud-and-
tube crenellated plastic blocks—the Lego Neuschwanstein (236,000
bricks), great Sioux chief Sitting Bull (1.4 million), and a Legoland Mount
Rushmore (1.5 million, plus 40,000 pieces of Duplo). Legoland reinforces
Lego's wholesome essence, even making Disneyland—whose smallest
park is twice the size of Legoland—seem almost noirish. (There are no
earthquakes or collapsed freeways at Legoland.)

Visitors who have paid dearly to stroll among the Lego pirates and medieval knights, the Lego Amsterdam townhouses and the Taj Mahal, the Lego Rhone River barges and mini-Bergen, Norway, with its tiny funicular railway, and the Lego Statue of Liberty, leave feeling more connected and loyal to the family-friendly company. They also leave many kroner lighter, for in the coarsest terms, Legoland is a prelude to the sale. "It is one magnificently large welcome mat to the store," says Carat Brand Experience chief Dale Tesmond, who at a previous company worked to breathe life into Legolands at Carlsbad and Windsor. While audiences for brand experiences are relatively small, they're very deep. "After people spend real time with you—sometimes as much as a day—they move up the relationship ladder from regular user or even loyalist to brand ambassador," says Tesmond.

For all its marketing impact, Legoland might just as well be called Logoland. Visitors follow its figurative yellow brick roads to a shop at the exit. Almost all carry their warm feelings about the company to cash registers back home. And that is why Lego has sold more than 200 billion of its standard bricks since 1958 and become the leading maker of construction toys in the world and the third-largest toy manufacturer overall. There are another 11 billion oversized Duplo bricks (introduced for toddlers in 1969) in toy bins worldwide. More than 300 million kids have owned Lego sets and 68 million do at this moment.

Early on, the architects of Legoland knew that consumers hunger to "feel" a product versus just hear about it. More women and Generation Ys of both genders say that experiencing a product or service, especially in a way that's entertaining, is far more likely to move them to buy it than any other marketing influence. And 9 out of 10 adults say that participating in a live event for a product or brand makes them more receptive to ads about it. Participants of a marketing experience recall the brand much more than if exposed in another way. Indeed, unlike TV commercials, experiences are permission based, even sought, and there's the likelihood or at least the possibility of real conversation with a brand representative instead of an imposed monologue.

People's receptivity to event marketing—at a time when they're increasingly closing the door to other forms of marketing—is why spending on it alone topped $166 billion in the United States in 2005, according to estimates from the trade publication *Promo*. That doesn't include sampling, games, contests and sweepstakes, sponsorships, or rolling billboards like the Oscar Mayer Wienermobile, which, 65 years after it first chugged along America's highways, still attracts crowds.

It also doesn't include the millions of dollars spent on gift bags, from celebrity goodies at the Oscars to takeaways for ordinary folks at charity events, or premiums and other keepsakes, or themed restaurants or hotel rooms (think Ian Schrager), or retail environments like the much-ballyhooed Stew Leonard's dairy store and American Girl doll store, or even museums like the Boeing-supported Future of Flight or the Mormon Temple interactive display that brings the story of its religion to life.

And it doesn't take into account the billions invested in corporate meetings and trade shows and other business-to-business events, exhibits, and environments, like where Caterpillar competitor JCB has six "dancing diggers" perform, or at the Honeywell Tech Center across from the Capitol Building where General Services Administration (GSA) purchasing agents can get hands-on demonstrations of avionics equipment. In other words, it's a large slice of an enormous pie.

And it's why Best Buy toured its Ultimate Dorm Room to colleges during back-to-school season. In it were monitors and PlayStation 2s tethered to the ceiling above a bunk bed, a mini-fridge, PCs and printers, and movies running on a plasma screen: everything a sophomore at Northwestern University would crave. The branded bus that Best Buy used to ferry students from campus to its nearest store was similarly bedecked with home entertainment systems, videogame pods, glass desktop computer stations, and MP3 listening stations.

The good feelings that morph into sales that are generated by experiential marketing prompted Maxim to open branded lounges to bring a *Maxim* experience to the party circuit. It's why Firefly Mobile launched its cell phone for kids (there's no keypad, just a direct-dial to Mom, Dad, and a few others the parents have programmed in), where families could try out the colorful glowing phone and receive free branded glowsticks and foam bats in the "Glow Room" at Major League Baseball games. And it's why Disney planted a 25 × 25 foot snowglobe in Times Square to promote the premiere of its *Chronicles of Narnia: The Lion, the Witch and the Wardrobe* film: A walk through the globe was like going through a magic wardrobe that simulates snowfall in Narnia.

Stores, too, are intensely receptive to these environments and events. While Bob Connolly (when chief marketing officer of Wal-Mart) once said, "We're not the marketing. We're the market," he urged suppliers to come up with "retailtainment" ideas, such as visits by "Axe Angels" sampling teams or Suave-sponsored game shows to play out in, or around, its stores. Coty Beauty parks its red double-decker bus in Wal-Mart parking lots to dispense actual or virtual makeovers (brand reps digitally add different shades to a computer image of the guest's face) and a printed list of the Rimmel cosmetics the makeup artists used. In 2005, the stores saw those printed lists boost cosmetic sales 32 percent. VIZ Media set up a mobile 92-seat theater outside Wal-Mart stores to give core consumers a sneak peek at the hotly anticipated release of *Inuyasha The Movie 3: Swords of an Honorable Ruler.* Theatergoers could buy the anime DVD in Wal-Mart. And to support the release of *Star Wars: Episode III* licensed products, samplers distributed more than 3.5 million products for Hasbro, Frito-Lay, M&M Mars, Pepsi, and Kellogg's at 400 Wal-Mart parking lots.

Rather than taking their show on the road to everywhere, companies spend a lot of energy figuring out the map to get some face time with their best prospects. Bosch Power Tools understood that tool touches equal sales, so it takes three 30-foot workshops on wheels to industrial job sites, trade shows, and motocross and NASCAR races as well as parking lots at category-killer hardware stores like Home Depot and Lowe's. Radio Shack tours its tuner radio control cars to skate parks. Whole Foods impregnates Lamaze classes to teach pregnant women what foods to avoid and how to prepare smoothies for baby. Equal's mobile café stops at lifestyle events where staffers serve Equal-laced coffee and tea and hand out custom-published Zagat travel guides with the top spots for brewed beverages. As part of its "Pick Your Own Stinkin' Prize," Yoo-hoo steered a tricked-out garbage truck (painted in Yoo-hoo colors, with a party lounge atop) to concerts. And Procter & Gamble brings its Therma-Care heat wraps to PGA Tournaments, gardening clubs, ski resorts— wherever people experience pain.

The slopes, however, with their monied and passionate skiers and snowboarders, are a lot more about pleasure than pain. And these days they're a lot about marketing and sampling. M&M/Mars reps hand out free Snickers at lift ticket windows. SoBe Beverages sponsors a super-pipe area at Okemo Mountain in Ludlow, Vermont, and American Express has a namesake main lift at nearby Stratton Mountain. Anheuser-Busch hosts the Bud Light Cowboy Downhill competition at Steamboat, and skiers at Vail can avail themselves of free Volvos after seeing a vehicle cutaway at the top of the main gondola run. At the Jeep King of the Mountain pro skiing and snowboarding competition, racers come out of a gate designed to look like the grille of a Jeep, and Volvo plants its cars as well as full-size models made of Lego blocks (it's a Legoland sponsor) all over mountains at ski resorts to enhance its family-friendly image. Charles Schwab rewards those who open new accounts with at least $100,000 in deposits with free ski lessons, lift tickets, and vacations.

Because people have demonstrated how willing they are to trade their undivided attention for free perks, some marketers have taken to offering unexpected, valuable services to prospects—and pitching them when they're down. Since 2000, Archer Daniels Midland has done free bone-density screenings outside pharmacies across the country to promote Novasoy, its soy isoflavones included in many dietary supplements. To push its Koala Fit-grips, Procter & Gamble–trained pros show up at day-care centers to make sure that car seats for children are safely installed. While doing the inspection they simultaneously talk up the new diapers and dispense cents-off coupons for them. Motorola got Chicago office workers to sit for free shoe shines—administered with a spiel about its wireless products.

Research suggests that event marketing works best for food and beverages, computers and other software, cell phones, and cars. Automakers find it's a great way to get a car noticed without making potential buyers feel the pressure they do in a showroom. Women are particularly open to interacting with household and healthcare gizmos. Interestingly, participants are likelier to immerse themselves in a marketing experience showcasing a product that they've heard of but never tried, than one that they already use.

Crafting an event, environment, or exhibit around a brand can bring even the dullest to life. The key, of course, is to make it fun and theatrical. "People choose to be there because they want to be blown away," says Tesmond. Citibank tried to blow them away and tout its ThankYou Network that differentiates its checking account when it touched down for three days at New York's Grand Central Terminal with skill games, mechanical surfboards, and sumo wrestlers. Passersby who got a hole-in-one at their miniature golf green (set up near a range of golf products available from Citi's ThankYou rewards catalog) won a $10 gift card to use at such retailers as Starbucks, Best Buy, and Barnes & Noble. Those who shot a certain number of baskets in a minute at the temporary basketball station received a $5 gift card. And those who hung on to its mechanical surfboard for a minute also got a $5 gift card. Citi set up mini-versions of the event at 10 of its financial centers around the city.

Bank of America also chose heavily traveled Grand Central to build a tangible experience around the intangible benefits of feeding even peanuts to a savings account. For three hours one afternoon, several hundred passersby clambered onto a cushy 750-pound red couch it had installed here to dig for "spare change" among its cushions. (Actually they were colorful tokens that these urban archeologists could trade for gift cards to Starbucks, the Apple Computer Store, and even mass-transit subway and bus rides.)

Sometimes the event is so theatrical that it becomes more stunt or spectator sport than participant immersion. To launch Virgin Mobile cellular service and its "Nothing to hide" pricing (no hidden fees or contracts), *The Full Monty* cast took it all off in Times Square—except for strategically placed cell phones. Virgin's showman CEO, Richard Branson, joined in the striptease aboard a giant cell phone hung in front of the company's Virgin Megastore there. (Other marketers, like Visa, have molded Broadway to suit their purposes. In 2002, Visa sponsored the Great White Way's *Movin' Out*, and gave its cardholders six weeks of advanced access to ticket sales. And for the show's national tour, Visa was the sole credit card accepted.)

Still, two of every three of the more than $13 billion spent on sponsorship programs in North America in 2005 went into sports, according to the Chicago-based sponsorship research and analysis firm IEG. Twenty-five years ago, the epitome of sports marketing was planting a big sign in the outfield, inviting customers to the game, and handing out T-shirts to create walking billboards. That evolved into CEOs directing their marketing teams to sponsor a sport about which they were passionate so they could snag the best seats. And that grew into experiential marketing events, like BellSouth's sponsorship of the PGA Tour since 1989. Its part-entertainment, part-demo BellSouth Interactive Zone lets fans take a five-minute video golf lesson and use other BellSouth products in the midst of sport-induced euphoria when there are lulls in the action and when they arrive early to get a good parking spot or hang around for traffic to clear. In a recent year, about 9 percent of the 20,000 visitors bought a product or services on the spot and more than 70 percent learned about one they might buy. The coup de grace for BellSouth was the global media coverage it got for donating the more than $11 million in tournament proceeds to Children's Healthcare of Atlanta.

Sponsoring the PGA Tour, or a sport like it, however, costs a fortune. It's not a build-it-and-they-will-come proposition so much as build-an-environment-so-tantalizing-that-people-will-line-up-to-come, and that's often expensive. Marketers are also required to buy spots on the TV shows that broadcast the event. And if they want to leverage or line-extend that sponsorship—otherwise, why do it?—*ka-ching* again. It can be costly in other ways too: ExxonMobil came under fire from some of its shareholders for sponsoring the Masters at the men's-only Augusta National Golf Club.

To cuts their costs and heighten their draw, some marketers have joined forces at some events. To woo Gen-Xtreme, that is, boys and young men who love skateboarding, BMX biking, motocross, and all other action sports that could result in a quick ticket to the emergency room, Pepsi's bright-yellow caffeine-infused soft drink, Mountain Dew, conceived the Dew Action Sports Tour. Here it constructs The House of Dew, where sponsored skateboarders hang out to interact with fans. There's also a Napster lounge to download tunes from their favorite athlete's play lists, a PlayStation2 room, (temporary) tattoo parlor, and a product-sampling kitchen.

Panasonic research found that when kids aren't on their skateboards and dirt bikes, they're watching action sports DVDs or dreaming about making their own videos. So, in Panasonic's Hi-Def Experience hands-on technology clinics on the Dew Action Sports Tour, bikers, boarders, and action sport fans learn how to shoot, edit, and manipulate footage with the brand's camcorders and digital cameras. Sports shoe maker Vans drives its RV there so fans can design a custom pair of Vans sports shoes in its Internet kiosk, and purchase them. DC Comics' *MAD* magazine shows up with free magazines and *MAD* artists drawing caricatures. "Consumers who are growing up on games, themed restaurants, and three-D won't stand for Two-D marketing," says Tesmond. "They support marketers who live and breathe their passion." This Peanut Chews tried to do with its museum of different boards to demo its knowledge of skate and surf. In addition to stoking up on the Chews, kids could have their photo taken so it looks like they're doing stunts on BMX bikes. Fans retrieved those pictures online, furnishing Peanut Chews with an online database of loyal customers.

Everyone loves getting something for nothing, so it's no surprise that people like to try something new with no financial risk. Marketers like dishing out samples because they work like nothing else to get someone to try a product (and very often, subsequently buy it). A year after male models went into offices to hand out samples of Hugo Boss fragrances, 72 percent of recipients remembered the scent fondly, without any prompting, and 58 percent had told someone else about the experience. Thirty-one percent had actually gone out to buy the fragrance.

That's why for years Neutrogena has been putting sample sizes of its glycerine soap in hotel bathrooms and why Butler plies dentists with toothbrushes to pass on to their patients. It's why Clorox has installed disinfecting-wipes dispensers next to shopping carts at supermarkets (so you can clean up after the shopper who used your cart previously) and why Unilever put *its* new antibacterial wipes on popcorn bags at movie theater concession stands.

Target Marketing & Research Inc., a Huntington, New York sampling company, found men prefer hand-delivered samples, whereas women prefer those that come in the mail. Companies spent over two billion dollars on product sampling in 2005, with more samples handed out in person at events. Sampling has become almost a requisite part of any product launch, but it's also used to seduce nonusers into the fold for an existing product, or get regular buyers to use the product in new ways. But sampling has evolved from simply handing out the goods on street corners to aiming to make an emotional connection. Ben & Jerry's set its sampling stage with a massive hot-air balloon and guerrilla visits to office buildings to scoop out free serves. And Baskin-Robbins distributed sweet incentives on Valentine's Day—a free scoop of its Love Potion No. 31 ice cream— to anyone dressed as Cupid.

The trick of sampling is to go where (and when) people are most open to being marketed to: lunchtime in the streets, festivals on weekends, and venues where the product naturally fits. Hall's stocks bins in theater lobbies with its cough drops, and Campbell's Soup dishes out chilis and soups at tailgating parties during football season. Dunkin' Donuts took its zero-fat Latte Lite drink to more than 200 health clubs, and during the NBA's All-Star Weekend, McDonald's recruited Denver Nuggets star Carmello Anthony and basketball Hall-of-Famer Bill Walton to hand out samples of its Chicken Selects strips at its Denver locations. The Meow Mix Café, a 3,500 square-foot pop-up store on Fifth Avenue and Forty-second Street in Manhattan, distributed 14,000 Wet Pouches in the 12 days it was up, and invited cats and their human companions to play interactive games.

Harlequin has Bed & Breakfasts plop one of its Intrigue books onto pillows during turndown service. Chattem Corp. puts samples of its Phisoderm Acne Clean Swab in gift packs at cheerleader camps. And GlaxoSmithKline has stewards on Carnival ships insert a two-tablet pouch of its Tums Cool Relief tablets in passengers' gift packs in their rooms. After all, who more likely than the cruising set to overindulge?

17

Why You Can't Find a Cell Phone Just for Talking

I n horror-novelist Stephen King's 2006 book, *Cell*, it's not avian flu or a chemical bomb that delivers the apocalypse to America. The devastating microwave energy pulse is delivered through cell phones, which wipe clean the brains of users, substituting uncontrollable aggressive and destructive impulses. The hero, comic book illustrator Clayton Riddell, and a small group of "normies," fight to survive amid chaos and carnage.

But even as the best-selling scaremonger crows on the book jacket that he doesn't own a cell phone and disdains them, his savvy publisher Simon & Schuster knows that the rest of the world feels differently. Their publicists blasted voicemail messages to the cell phones of more than 100,000 fans with King uttering "Beware. The next call you take may be your last," or "It's okay, it's a normie calling" to incite them to buy the book.

King and his publisher aren't the only ones who've got your number. In spring 2006, Toyota launched its cheeky new Yaris with ads on conventional TV and radio, in magazines and MySpace.com (where it claims more than 38,000 "friends"), as part of a video game ("Evolution Fighting"), and on that business-card-sized gadget nestled in your purse or back pocket.

In an attempt to sell 18-to-34-year-olds on the mischievousness of its new sedan, the automaker glommed onto one of that age group's favorite shows: Fox's *Prison Break*, about a guy who commits a crime to land in the big house so he can spring his falsely imprisoned brother. Its seven 10-second commercials in which a cartoonish Yaris takes on *Matrix*-like machinery are cute, but it's *where* Toyota ran them that's interesting: before two-minute mobisodes of *Prison Break: Proof of Innocence*, available to owners of Sprint mobile phones who've purchased a video package.

Fox had invented the word *mobisode*, meaning an episode of a TV show shown on a mobile phone, the year before. Then it had released "24: Conspiracy," 24-minute inspirations from the hot TV series using different writers and a different cast (per union laws then that have since changed). Fox was unhappy with the production and dropped it after one season but "24: Conspiracy" prompted the creation of a new Emmy Award category and launched an enduring concept. In late 2004, Fox aired 60-second mobisodes of 24 in a dozen European countries and Japan on Vodafone.

The newly paved road Toyota drove helps explain why you'll have a hard time finding a new cell phone just for talking. Mobile carriers have plowed billions of dollars into enhancing their headsets (read: content and advertising delivery systems) and getting them into your pockets. The reason is that there's money to be made here from premium services, lots of it.

Consider that cell phone owners around the world forked over $12 billion in 2005 (according to the Yankee Group) just for ringtones and wallpaper (the graphic on your screen). And that in just its first six months, Apple's video iPod sold 15 million video downloads, with programs like *Lost* and *The Office* suggesting that even if it's only sharp young eyes doing the downloading, lots of them are doing it lots of the time. Consider how briskly Motorola's Razr ($199) and Palm's Treo ($399) have sold, and the way these status symbols are casually whipped out or positioned on conference tables during meetings.

Cell phones are as widely owned as wallets; worldwide they outsell computers six to one. Analysts expect that by 2010 there'll be four billion of them out there. While it takes the average guy two days to discover he's lost his credit card, it only takes him five minutes to realize his cell phone has gone missing. To young people, they're more than a flip-up screen to glance at while waiting for the train or wandering the mall: They are their fashion statement, virtual hangout, life organizer, and personal communication oxygen.

ABI Research predicts that the worldwide market for roving-screen-TV will reach $27 billion by 2010. Others think that's conservative. The United States represents a relatively thin slice of that because only around 40 million of the 214 million cell phones here are currently video-capable. Most cell phone users upgrade their phone every 18 months. In 2005, 370 million people worldwide carried camera phones; by 2006 it was twice that number, says research firm InfoTrends/CAP Ventures in Weymouth, Massachusetts.

Based on how Asians and Europeans have embraced the third screen, marketers know it will be more than talk on these shores, too. For example, while 39 percent of Asians and 36 percent of Europeans had received a text message ad by 2006, just 8 percent of Americans had (though 65 percent were open to it). Eighty-three percent of Japanese have cell phones with gizmos, as do 52 percent of Western Europeans and 60 percent of Chinese and South Koreans—and they're content to watch long-form TV on it—even those beyond adolescence. No one expected many would watch TV episodes on their iPods either, but no one can doubt that they do.

Carriers are expanding the market beyond the young and restless who are most likely to snap cell phone pics and buy ring tones by cozying up to other low-hanging fruit. For example, they're pushing hard to attract Hispanics, who tend to use lots of pricey data services and spend 975 minutes a month on their phones, double what Caucasians do, according to market research firm Telephia.

Although the United States is some 18 months behind the rest of the world in cell phone terms, it all began in these parts. In 1947, Bell Laboratories introduced cell phones as part of police car technology. The system (actually a type of two-way radio) uses many base stations to divide a service area into multiple cells, which are transferred from one base station to another as a user travels from cell to cell. But it was a Motorola scientist, Dr Martin Cooper, who is credited with inventing the first totally portable handset in 1973. Bell then built a prototype cell system and tested it in Chicago in 1977. (Separately in 1979, the first commercial cell phone system began operation in Tokyo.) By 1982, after much foot dragging, the FCC authorized commercial cell service. Five years later, more than one million subscribers in America had signed on. The first American mobile video service began in late 2003, when Sprint offered a choppy TV extract. Two years later, MTV's VH1 and Comedy Central and ABC and ESPN began offering clips of existing TV shows through American carriers like Verizon. Then MTV began editing for the screen with scenes excised from shows like *Punk'd* and *The Shop*.

The cinderblock phones of yesteryear have given way to mere bricks, and ultimately, lightning-fast, razor-thin handsets. The main play is still voice and text communication. But newer devices come with so many features (speakers, high-speed Internet, small but usable keyboards, enhanced memory and expansion slots for even more, and battery life to download and play albums, video games, and TV shows) that it's regarded as a chip-techno Swiss Army Knife.

So far, most video content on cell phones has been news headlines, sports scores and highlights, music videos, stand-up comedy, talking-head shows, and, of course, porn. Watching it has been likened more to ham radio than the digital revolution. Because the screens are a tiny two-inches-by-two-inches max, "filming to the phone" means lots of eye-catching close-ups and brightly colored backgrounds so characters pop. Zooming, panning, and quick movement blurs the image: Video streams at 15 frames a second, half the rate of regular television. (With only 160 characters including spaces to work with, text or SMS [short message service] has its own severe limitations.) And because downloading big blocks consumes memory and airtime, most cell phone programming is short "snack video."

Initially, broadcasters reckoned that the snack would whet viewers' appetites for the real meal, the TV show, and that it would extend the brand and foster loyalty. Soon they realized that viewers were doing more than time shifting; they were place shifting and they carried these teeny screens everywhere and turned to them while watching TV, listening to the radio, or staring at a billboard—in short, superseding other media. Only then did mobile content become its own narrowcast, deserving of original content rather than repurposed TV fare.

While we wish they'd deal with banishing dropped calls first, carriers have joined all manner of traditional and nontraditional content providers in a furious wireless gold rush. CBS made an original soap opera for the smallest screen, as well as versions of *CBS News to Go* and *Entertainment Tonight*, branded "ET to Go" as a nod to the truncated format. Fox set up Mobizzo, a one-stop online shop for cell-phone entertainment, sold mobile episodes of reality genre, *The Simple Life*, and created 26 one-minute originals of *Love and Hate* and *The Sunset Hotel* for Verizon's V CAST. It also let phonies text vote for *American Idol*. In 2004, more than 13 million had voted by cell phone.

Cingular customers watched HBO on their phones, ESPN let Sprint subscribers get sports, news, and interviews with athletes, and Sprint-Nextel users caught live Major League Baseball games. Verizon customers could catch mini-moments from *Lost*, and *Friends* still lived on, on cell phones. NBC Universal TV head Jeff Zucker promised that all new programs on the network would be available through cell phones, computers, or iPods.

Independent producers created a futuristic series starring Dennis Hopper for small screens and the young male-oriented web site Heavy.com pushes some of its perverse content onto the mobile screen. MTV, which calls itself the world's largest mobile-content provider, created the first domestic made-for-cell series, *Sway's Hip-Hop Owner's Manual*. Its Comedy Central hosts *Samurai Love God*, an original animated mobile series voiced by *Daily Show* correspondent Ed Helms and adult-film star Jenna Jameson, and eight mobisodes of *Head and Body*, comic sketches in which a man with a detached head tries to keep it with his body. And it recently green-lighted a computer-animated made-for-mobile show comprised of funny interactions between walking, talking avatars of acne, vomit, gas, small breasts, and pubic hair, that is, the alter-egos of young teens.

Music is where MTV cut its TV teeth, and mobile ones, too. Music is the lifeblood of cell phone content. In addition to ringtones and full-song downloads, that includes music videos, promos around rock concerts, interviews with stars, and sneak peaks of future releases. The punk-pop Yellowcard quintet hit it big with its first album, based on conventional radio and CD sales. The band hit it bigger with its second album, launched exclusively on cell phone. Its title song, "Lights and Sounds," became the centerpiece soundtrack for commercials promoting Verizon's music download service.

Just as radio once introduced sounds to record-buying audiences, cell phones are now *the* springboard to CD sales, wooed by labels and artists for exposure. Songs from rapper T.I.'s album, *King*, aired on Sprint Nextel before it was sold anywhere. Sony released Shakira's "Hips Don't Lie" initially as a Verizon commercial. And Madonna's "Hung Up" was heard on cell phone commercials and as a ringtone before it was heard on the radio. Even though with new technology you can click, sample, and buy music from a phone, rapper T-Pain and others sell more songs as ringtones than as singles or albums.

Hollywood also recognizes that to young people who've never known a world without wireless, cell phones are both entertainment center and portal to more. That is why, to drive ticket-buyers to the box office, in summer 2006, on a mini-screen near you was playing behind-the-scenes production diaries, ring tones and wallpaper images, and streams of film clips and trailers from *Poseidon*, *Pirates of the Caribbean: Dead Man's Chest*, *Mission Impossible III*, and *Superman Returns*.

For some time, guys have used their cell phones to play games—the video kind, too. On Sprint phones, players of the interactive "Freestyle Mini" are transported to a virtual world, "Freestyle USA," to compete in races and contests. Their prize: karma points and bucks to soup up their vehicles. The game's continuing storyline is sent episodically to cell phones. And after the sultry star of Xbox's "Perfect Dark Zero" follows out your orders, she phones your cell to confirm the job is done.

But the killer app that has marketers salivating for this location-based medium is its portable interactivity. In fact, the next killer app coming down the mobile pike will be search. While search today is based on keywords, tomorrow it will be crossed with location, moving search from a research model to a concierge model. It's the difference between re-

searching who makes pizza and getting pizza right now. You can anticipate what will happen in cell phones by looking at navigation systems in
cars. They went from maps to maps with real-time road conditions coming over the Net via satellite radio receiver, that is, location-based services. Small, local businesses will make offers to people's mobiles in a
four-block radius based on their mobile search queries. That's one reason
why they've stampeded to register domain names ending in dot.mobi.
(The .com or .org address doesn't chime with a phone.) Within hours on
the first day that Dublin-based Mobile Top Level Domain opened its registry, thousands of companies had signed up, including myyahoo.mobi,
Hotjobs.mobi, and chinamobile.mobi. P&G entered some 500 dot-mobi
sites, and movies and TV shows like *Family Guy*, and *The Matrix* staked out
their claims. Most had already stockpiled "short codes," those four- to six-
digit phone numbers to which phonies text message requests for information, sports scores, weather alerts, or electronic coupons, or to vote or
participate in contests.

Eighty-nine percent of major brands plan to market via mobile
phones by 2008, according to software company Airwide Solutions. And
more than half of them expect to spend between 5 and 25 percent of their
marketing budgets there in the next five years.

The welcome mat will be out for them. Even though airtime is getting cheaper (a minute now costs three to five cents, down from a quarter
or more a decade ago), and the average cell phone bill is only $40 to $50
a month with video services adding another $15 or so, consumers are
very willing to trade listening to ads for a discounted bill. They've shown
that on their landlines by dialing such directory services as 1-800-411-
SAVE to listen to ads in exchange for someone looking up the number for
free. That's not to say that advertisers will be buying lots of time on handsets any time soon, and we don't anticipate that mobile video will become
popular for at least five years, because it does not provide the social con-
nection/currency of the shared experience that TV or You Tube does. In
fact, no mobile service will succeed unless it fosters those elements, including Amp'd or ESPN mobile (which went from charging people $600
to sign up for the service, to six months later, paying them $600). Despite
gobs of money spent on them, their subscription rates are minuscule.

Helio, on the other hand, we expect will succeed because rather than ask users to take part in a new community, Helio proposes to enhance the user's current experience.

As phonies begin to feel digital sticker shock from small charges for new content mounting up, they'll be even more receptive to ads. In 2006, 83 percent told Go2 Networks that they'd rather have ads subsidize their cell phone addiction than reach into their own pockets to fund it. Go2 delivered more than 50 million cell phone ads last year for companies like Progressive Casualty Insurance. Virgin paid its participants a minute of talking time if they agreed to receive text messages on their phones and answer questions demonstrating that they were really paying attention. Despite their alleged contempt for advertising, mobile phone users are far likelier than the general public to act on it. Response rates are 4 to 10 percent compared with less than 1 percent for direct mailing or online advertising.

Other companies than Toyota have also experimented here. American Express motivated a demographic important to it to register for mobile alerts on the chance they'd win Land Rovers or plasma TVs. Corona got 15,000 people to opt-in for mobile messages about its products and events during Cinco de Mayo. ABN AMRO encourages customers to check balances, transfer funds, and pay bills via cell phone—shaving customer service costs for the bank. And Allstate underwrites the dissemination of college football rankings to subscribers of ESPN Phone's programs.

Burger King gave Sprint customers the opportunity to snag Super Bowl tickets if they text messaged in a code found on its Chicken Fries packaging. (It also provided "curtain calls" of its infamous Whopperettes commercial.) Jeep ran hourly ads on 18 MobiTV channels, and its own Jeep channel continuously played episodes of *The Mudds*, about an outdoorsy, mud-splattered family that drives a Jeep Commander. Nike text messages daily training tips to gym rats.

Marketers eager to gratify instantly have sent ads or offers to GPS-equipped cell phones based on their location. MasterCard approached cell phone owners looking for a place to eat with the chance to win free lunches at nearby restaurants. Others have taken advantage of RFID chips by urging consumers to, say, photograph their bar code in the supermarket and receive recipes, calorie counts, discount coupons, or a relevant gift in return. The image-recognition software can also help you decide whether to eat at the dive on the corner by furnishing reviews to the phone, or race to the movie by providing screening times.

Notwithstanding concerns with Anheuser-Busch for inadvertently enticing underage drinkers by advertising on MobiTV's 30 channels, the Mobile Marketing Association developed a voluntary code of conduct. Marketers who subscribe contact only those who've given permission. The dot-mobi domains won't "cause pop-ups or other windows to appear," and they've agreed to parse their pages into usable but limited size portions. Of course, carriers can't sell phone numbers to telemarketers or share information about a subscriber or his whereabouts. (For that matter, no phone company can share customer data with the government without a warrant.)

In addition to enticing advertisers, the third screen has also lured in the search engines. Google, Yahoo!, and Microsoft created software and deals so that their search engines and logos pop up on cell phones. Before, people *could* search on their phones, but surfing the Web there had been likened to surfing the Pacific on a tiny board, limited by sluggish downloads, tiny screens, and inadequate batteries. Now Internet connections are faster, screens are bigger and better, and search engines are tailoring results to the screen consumers carry in their pockets.

Mobile marketing and content-to-go are so alluring that in late 2005, eBay bought Luxembourg-based Skype Technologies for $2.6 billion and another $1.5 billion performance payout (at least 43 times its revenue). Skype, which lets users make free phone calls worldwide over the Internet, is a pioneer in the emerging click-to-call (really "click-to-be-called-back") arena. Click on an ad or logo, type in your phone number, and presto—you won't even have to ask if he can hear you now; the local plumber will be on the line telling you when he can get to your flooded basement.

Stephen King hijacked the power of cell phones by painting a demonic view of what can pulse through them. Charles Fritz, chairman of NeoMedia Technologies, has a more benign vision. In the not-so-distant future you won't just use your phone to call for tickets to a Rolling Stones concert: Your phone will become your ticket. Purchase one and a unique code will be sent to the phone that you'll wave before a scanner at the concert to gain entry. That's the kind of reaching out and touching we'd prefer.

18

WHY, THOUGH YOU'VE SIGNED UP ON THE DO-NOT-CALL REGISTRY, YOU'RE STILL BESIEGED BY TELEMARKETERS

Starting October 1, 2003, federal law required telemarketers to search the Federal Trade Commission/Federal Communications Commission's Do Not Call registry at least every three months and cross off any name registered there. A year later, some 110 million folks had signed up, and long after the time lag for prospects to be removed from the list many were still having dinner interrupted by telemarketers. The FTC concedes it fields 1,500 to 3,000 consumer complaints a day about junk calls.

Alas, there are as many loopholes as there are provisions to this regulation. Political organizations are exempt. So are most charities (unless those dialing are for-profit telemarketers). Survey companies get the green flag as long as they're not (obviously) trying to induce you to buy something. Calls to announce that your delivery is in, or your bill is due, are also fair game. And if you bought something (or made your last payment for it) within the last 18 months or had something delivered in that time frame, you're classified as an existing customer with a welcome-telemarketer-mat at your door. And if you rang up a company to inquire about a product or service on offer within the last three months, that company has carte blanche to ring you back, even if you are on the registry, unless you specifically instruct them not to.

In January 2006, the satellite TV provider DirectTV agreed to pay $5.3 million for having violated the Telephone Consumer Protection Act. And Ryan A. Swanberg, the high school dropout who wrote *Lawsuit: How I Turned the Tables on Telemarketers and Debt Collectors*, earns around $100,000 annually from challenging telemarketers who miss the letter of the law. Even that hasn't silenced the ringing.

Some telemarketers singled out by these roomy restrictions have resorted to ingenious dodges to keep the instrument Alexander Graham Bell devised in their service. Among our favorites are: "This is not a sales call"; "We have been trying to reach you to deliver your (free/ complimentary) (Best Buy gift card/$500,000 contest winnings/vacation to Orlando)"; and, of course, "Your call is important to us." The phones keep ringing because telemarketing pays. According to the FCC, telemarketers attempt 104 million calls a day and rake in more than $650 billion a year. Some $40 billion of that is from scams. The most fruitful ones, according to the National Fraud Information Center, involve guaranteed loan and credit offers and sweepstakes prizes, both of which require an advance fee.

In 2005, each dollar invested in direct marketing returned on average $11.49 in incremental revenue across all industries and $61 billion generated $1.85 trillion in sales—or 10.3 percent of the total U.S. gross domestic product (GDP). In 2006, direct marketing drove sales of $1.962 trillion. So mammoth is the potential here that in mid-2006 the Interpublic Group of Companies (IPG) folded its 133-year-old Foote Cone & Belding agency with its 100-plus office global network into direct marketing firm Draft. Gallup found that the only people the public trusts less than car salespeople are telemarketers; IPG found their profit-making trajectory too compelling.

Direct marketing is flourishing not only because it is transparently accountable, but because it's also extremely efficient. Dell may be in the soup now, but it got to the dessert table on the wings of direct marketing, or at least its progenitor company, PCs Ltd., did. In 1989, chubby, 22 year-old college dropout Michael Dell invited the Riney agency to take over the ads he and his friends had been cobbling together on the back of pizza boxes. With targeting mail, for instance, there's little wasted energy. Marketers can buy lists of exactly whom they want to reach. Are you targeting chief financial officers? Chessie Lists Inc. has a 32,840-name file you could rent for $70 per thousand names. How about people who responded to infomercials for children's products? For $90 per thousand you can have access to 219,417 of them through List Experts Inc. Are you looking for devotees of Christian music? They're yours, for just $95 per thousand names through Direct Partner Solutions Inc. Marketers after professionals who specialize in animals or plants can have their postal addresses for $245 per thousand, their telephone/fax numbers for $345 per thousand, and their e-mail addresses for $475 per thousand through the Bethesda List Center Inc. For those who recently bought a 30-day supply of vitamins it's 10 cents a name from Macromark Inc. Are you looking for buyers of male potency products? They are available for $110 per thousand names from Impulse Media.

Still, since the Do Not Call legislation tightened the phone cord, marketers have migrated to other direct marketing channels such as "junk" e-mail, catalogs, and direct-response TV. (For three years, Carat scored for DiTech here until it won the Hyundai business. General Motors, which owns DiTech, didn't like that and fired the agency.) Hooked-on-Phonics, which invented the "vanity phone number" (1-800-abc-defg) that has been widely copied (i.e., 1-800-mattres), proved that radio could be a powerful direct marketing channel. Current and evolving technology should make it even more powerful. Soon, when you hear a radio commercial in a car, you'll be able to push a button and automatically capture the information onto your mobile phone for later use.

Fuji Film abandoned the sitcom-like TV ads it once ran in favor of direct-response television commercials that propel viewers to a phone number or their web site. The traditional 30-second TV spots were too short to explain Fuji's technology. One- and two-minute direct-response ads gave it enough time to describe how the picture stabilization feature on its digital cameras makes pictures less blurry and backgrounds less murky.

Similar-length spots for its disposable cameras afford it time to explain, via picture-to-picture comparisons, why its 1,000-speed film bests the 400-speed film you get in most competing cameras.

Direct-response TV ads (which appear during off-demand times or in commercial slots that stations are having a hard time selling) have been getting the required audience or gross rating points for half the price (or less) of "normal" TV buys. Miraculously, in a world calculated on cost-per-lead, direct marketers are able to bottom-feed because they're actually looking for shows where viewers are less involved. It's why direct marketers love *Gilligan*, for example, because viewers are not too engrossed in it (as they'd be, say, in *60 minutes*) to respond to a pitch. Less-involving shows produce better direct-response rates. (Alas, this silver lining may disappear once the pause capability of a TiVo becomes universal.)

Now, companies like Invidi and Open TV are able to direct commercials to specific households, so that homes ruled by Morris and Tiger receive the Iams cat food spot while ones with Duke and Rover get the Iams dog food spot. Soon these direct-response ads will allow an interested viewer to "click here" for a brochure, or to be contacted by a sales rep, or to be linked to a web site. (After all, it's only "junk" if it's nothing you want. When you're in the market for something, discounts and advice are valuable.)

What Fuji has done, using other media to drive traffic to its transactional web site, is dead-on Generation III direct marketing (Gen III DM). Carat defines Gen III Direct Marketing as a combination of interactive and direct mail assets at the dawn of the digital, one-to-one marketplace. On Fuji's robust web site at the center of the marketing universe, consumers can browse if they're not ready to buy, buy when they're ready, talk to a real person if they want advice, or be directed to a brick-and-mortar store to experience the product first-hand.

Voice Over Internet Protocol (VOIP) takes this to the next level. An online searcher who wants to speak to a live person can be connected directly to the marketer's call center instead of their web site. Rising paper and postage costs are conspiring to railroad direct marketing to the Internet, but web data analysis is what makes this mine a gusher: Companies can direct their pitches based on a customer's past purchases.

The problem is, because e-mail is virtually free, many companies still scatterblast their offers. Even with the federal Can Spam Act, and several high-profile federal prosecutions against individual junk e-mailers, and filters that Internet service providers and e-mail services use to protect their users from a bombardment of unwanted mail, some 60 to 70 percent of the world's e-mail is *unsolicited commercial e-mail (UCE)*. (*Wired* magazine puts it at 87 percent.) The term *spam* actually came from British comedy team Monty Python's "Spam" skit, performed in a restaurant that served almost nothing but the funny-named canned meat.

Spam is omnipresent. A University of Maryland study estimated that American businesses spend $22 billion a year in employee time deleting it. And it is insidious. Like a virus, it keeps cropping up despite armies of practitioners bent on its destruction. People change account names or even pretend to have died to outrun it. Filters to catch it get increasingly sophisticated. Microsoft's Sender ID confirms the true origin of an e-mail, making it harder for spammers to hide. Blue Security's Blue Frog creates fake addresses ("honeypots") to trap spammers. And legal clampdowns are getting toothier. For example, federal law bans misleading subject lines, including anything disguised to look as if it's from someone known to the recipient. (Spam often pretends to be from a real person.) Studies show users check the "from" column on their e-mail even before they check the subject line.

Yet this is a game of one-upmanship, and spammers get ever nimbler dodging these bullets. They engage in smart marketing, of course: firing off blasts between Tuesdays and Thursdays, 11 a.m. to 2 P.M., for instance, when more e-mail is opened than at any other time. (On the other hand, how smart is it to (a) alienate your audience, or (b) suggest that if you've got money to waste on ill-targeted solicitations you don't really need their contributions?)

Sometimes they cross the ethical divide. They hide themselves or their operations in countries with lax law enforcement (like Russia, China, and Nigeria). They use zombie bots—vast networks of surreptitiously captured personal computers that have been infected with malicious software so that they spew get-rich-quick schemes and pitches for penis-enlargement pills under the user's name. The FTC figures zombies deliver half to three-quarters of all spam. And they try to dupe the antispam filters. They intentionally misspell words or use images instead of triggering language to get past filters, and string seemingly random words together to catch your attention.

Spam scrubbers have prompted some marketers to practice so-called list hygiene. The Leukemia and Lymphoma Society recently slashed its e-mail list from 33,636 addresses to 4,510 after it discovered that its quarterly newsletters were being blocked as spam for almost a third of its subscribers. Reluctantly, it resought permission from its entire e-mail list. Happily for the Society, spam complaints subsequently disappeared, the average percent of people opening their communications more than doubled, and the clickthrough rate more than tripled. The net result was that even with a sharply pared list their total clicks per campaign were virtually unchanged.

On the other hand, an overly eager filter zapped as spam Elite Telecom Services' follow-up to a bid that would have saved the Cobb County schools in Georgia at least $250,000 in systemwide telephone services. Part of the filter that watches for porn was tripped by the inoffensive term "long distance."

Fax spam has also been disallowed. Until 1990, junk faxes were a routine form of advertising. The 1991 Telephone Consumer Protection Act outlawed anyone in the United States from faxing an ad without the recipient's prior express invitation or permission. The penalty was steep (at least $500 for every offense), but not until lawyers saw the potential from class action suits did it become effective. In 2001, a Georgia court ordered Hooters restaurant to pay $11.9 million for faxing unsolicited ads. (Some $3.9 million went to attorneys' fees.) Other states have also ruled that unlawfully converting the recipients' toner and paper for marketers' own use violates the right of privacy. The FCC's Junk Fax Prevention Act of 2005 spells it out more concretely.

While the nonprofit Center for a New American Dream has been (so far, futilely) lobbying Congress to establish a "Do Not Junk" mail registry, it's more the market forces that have been battering direct mail. More than 100 billion pieces of it flowed through the Post Office in 2006. Many were personalized or disguised as something else. Cingular Wireless, for example, sent out what looked like a wedding invitation when it merged with AT&T Wireless. Others look like holiday cards with handwritten addresses and personalized stamps. Others go the "Urgent" route, braying "Important Information Enclosed." Some envelopes mimic government agencies—real or fictitious. A mimic of the U.S. Department of Housing and Urban Development with a "rate overpayment notification" turns out to be a refinancing solicitation. Ditto a yellow letter with a Statue of Liberty symbol and the "United States of America" in Gothic print on the envelope.

Those 100 billion pieces may turn out to have been the industry's weightiest. Hefty postage rate increases went into effect in 2006. Paper costs climbed some 8 percent that year. And people are paying less attention to their mailboxes because the amount of personal or critical communications in them has fallen sharply. Consider, for example, how many people bank online. In 2005, the response rate to financial services mailings fell 46 percent, according to the Direct Marketing Association.

What this means for catalogs is that some will get slimmer, others will get juicier, and most will have as their prime mission corralling traffic to the web sites. Catalogs are great for browsing, the direct mail doyenne Lillian Vernon once noted. But selling on the Web is more targeted and efficient. (She means for the company: Using a mouse to "flip" virtual pages of a catalog can be time consuming and clumsy.) Today, Vernon's Internet presence accounts for about one-fourth of the company's total orders. For L.L. Bean, another famous cataloger, it's more than a half.

For a long time, marketers evaluated their catalogs by a "square-inch analysis"—that is, how much space generated how much revenue. In the 1980s, specialty retailers like Williams-Sonoma and Patagonia began including editorials in their pages (recipes and climbing, hiking, and environmental issues respectively). Spiegel's first catalog appeared in 1905. A recent 400-page, two-pound "magalog" or "catazine" was far from that nuts-and-bolts type of publication. Chockablock with feature stories about products it offers, its cover featured a scantily clad lass cuddling her catalog while her half-naked guy dozes nearby under a leopard-skin throw.

Americans receive almost 18 billion catalogs a year; in the last 12 months, 167 million people (women more so than men) ordered more than $150 billion worth of stuff from them. The most popular stuff by far is clothes (although that has been dropping), followed by gifts, books, music CDs and videos, home furnishings, and electronics. Tools are the fastest growing category.

Even as some catalogs fade out, newcomers continually join the 10,000-or-so flock out there. The first mail-order business, Montgomery Ward's, started in 1872 and stopped shipping a catalog in 1985. Sears, Roebuck closed its legendary Big Book catalog in 1993 after a 100-year run. On the other hand, Hasbro launched its first shop-at-home catalog in March 2006, and Home Depot recently added a second catalog, 10 Crescent Lane, a fictional address symbolizing a classic American neighborhood.

Alas, those classic American neighborhoods are becoming increasingly hard for direct marketers to penetrate. (Or to get paid for penetrating: A huge problem in direct marketing is slippage—the number of leads that come in but aren't "qualified." My former client Arrowhead saw its home water delivery service attracted lots of migrant workers who ordered the water service, received it for a few months, and never paid for it.) New "no knock" lists bar people from going door to door to peddle goods or ideas. In towns that have adopted them, door-to-door solicitors receive copies of the no-knock lists; residents post signs indicating they are on it, and police departments maintain and enforce the lists with jail terms and fines. Let's see how they get around that one.

19

Why You Won't Have a Clue That General Motors Is Behind That Blog

A malicious "Dear Steven" letter posted on a billboard in mid-Manhattan caught more than Steven's attention. "I know all about her, you dirty, sneaky, immoral, unfaithful, poorly endowed slimeball," it ranted. "Everything's caught on tape. Your (soon-to-be-ex) wife, Emily."

Good Morning America invited "Emily" on, *British Glamour* tried to profile her, and throughout blogville, antennae went up. Bloggers dug in and quickly deduced that billboards identical to this one beamed over Brooklyn, Los Angeles, and Chicago, and Emily, rather than the victim of cheating husband Steven, was the fictitious persona behind thatgirl emily.blogspot.com.

Faster than you could mutter *blogosphere*, the denizens of this new world also nailed the source and rationale behind the stunt. Court TV was promoting a new reality show, *Parco P.I.* Even uncloaked as a publicity ploy, Emily's blog reeled them in (one million visited); a phony surveillance scene from it became one of YouTube's most-viewed videos.

In the dark ages at the end of the twentieth century, corporations ran ads and bloggers blogged. Then, as companies increasingly saw their interruptive advertising wasn't penetrating, they ventured into the unknown territory of online journals where readers join in a back-and-forth conversation and where the chatter had become too loud to ignore.

At the close of 2002, there were some 15,000 blogs worldwide. In June 2006, more than 34 million had sprung up. More than 100 new blogs start every minute—roughly two each second. Their number has doubled every 5.5 months over the past three years, according to the Technorati search engine. If this growth spurt were to continue unchecked, all 6.7 billion people on the planet would have a blog by April 2009.

No topic is verboten and no excuse for a blog too trivial. Name a subject (other than yourself) and chances are there's already a blog devoted to it. Instapundit.com is a blog magnet for conservatives and dailykos.com for liberals. Beyond politics, blogs meander into everything from teeth to toenails, the Los Angeles Dodgers and Los Angeles dogs. Bloggers could be navel-gazers or soapbox activists. By one account, 9 out of 10 blogs are either abandoned soon after baptism or updated too infrequently to qualify as the genuine article. By another, 55 percent of blogs are still posting three months after they were created. Supposedly half are authored by teens, but more and more are birthed by businesses.

Under authoritarian regimes, such as in Iran where 41 daily newspapers were shut down in the past decade, the anonymity, spontaneity, and freewheeling ways of blogs let citizens weigh in on issues they'd have little access to otherwise. In open societies, where every blog is essentially its own printing press, the profusion makes for a overload of data. Many consider it an avalanche of irrelevance.

Marketers, however, consider it media that is finely, almost surgically sliced, the answer to their dream of selling Polygrip to the toothless. Because bloggers often talk about what they like and dislike, a cat-food company, say, can zero in on the feline-focused. And even though advertising inventory (freed from limitations of the page and the clock) is virtually infinite—and thus cheap—advertisers willingly pay more for highly targeted sites that are relevant for and interesting to the blog's audience.

According to thetruthlaidbear.com, only two blogs get more than one million visitors a day. After that it's off the cliff: No traffic jams block the 10th-ranked blog, which gets on average only 120,000 visits a day. Traffic reports of the 50th most popular site suggests around 28,000 visitors a day, while the 100th most visited gets fewer than 10,000.

The fractionalization of blogs belies their power. Blogs have been a catalyst in several current events. Gossip-blog Gawker's report about a cocaine epidemic on Wall Street touched off a crusade in mainstream media (or what bloggers call "the lamestream media"). After it revealed that a young Republican staffer had blogged from her office about her many liaisons, including one with a married Bush administration official, Jessica Cutler was fired for misusing office property. (She did, however, promptly land a book deal and a *Playboy* photo spread.) During the 2004 Presidential election campaign, bloggers took down CBS's Dan Rather for going with what it turned out were fake memos about Bush's Texas Air National Guard service on *60 Minutes*.

Two years earlier, TalkingPointsMemo.com highlighted Trent Lott's segregationist remarks and 13 days later, under pressure, Lott resigned as Senate majority leader. In August 2006, the politically conservative blog, Little Green Footballs, revealed that photos from Israeli air strikes on Beirut were doctored. A Reuters photo with plumes of black smoke rising over the buildings in a way they don't naturally curl prompted blog proprietor Charles Johnson to expose it as "blatant evidence of manipulation."

Instead of running scared, almost all traditional media have jumped on the blog bandwagon. The *Atlanta Journal-Constitution* runs 57 blogs on its web site, covering such areas as local sports, entertainment, parenting, relationships, technology, and gardening. John Robinson, editor of the *News & Record* in Greensboro, North Carolina, instructed his reporters to turn themselves into bloggers, and he invited readers to act as reporters, filing their own stories. Not all big media gone blogging has come off seamlessly. When the *Los Angeles Times* let readers post on its page, porn popped up, and its invitation came down. Moviemakers know what blogs can do: *Snakes on a Plane* didn't sell as many tickets as NewLine Cinema had expected, but those expectations had been fueled by perhaps the most clever prerelease hype on the Internet of any movie ever. That was initiated by a blog (and by Carat, which bought the media) as the ultimate teaser campaign, a modern-day equivalent to Infiniti's infamous rocks and trees campaign. Samuel L. Jackson (and many a blogger in blogdom picking up his comments) fueled those flames by insisting the only reason he'd agreed to star in the flick was the title. The proposed *Venom* or *Pacific Air Flight 121*, just wouldn't do. Recognizing the buzz blogs had stirred up for what had been a minor movie in New Line's 2006 lineup, the company added footage to bring the movie in line with growing fan zeal, and a blog line that originated as a parody of Jackson's movie persona: "Enough is enough! I have had it with these muthaf—-in' snakes on this muthaf—-in' plane!"Other bloggers created songs, apparel, poster art, mock movie trailers, and even short film parody competitions that ran on Digg, iFilm, and YouTube. There was even a takeoff—*Snakes Who Missed the Plane*.

Despite how pervasive blogs are, in mid-2006, 62 percent of Americans weren't sure exactly what a blog was, according to the Pew Internet and American Life Project. That's not entirely surprising when you consider that blogs didn't even exist before 1994, when Swarthmore student Justin Hall created what's believed to be the first, Links.net. It wasn't until three years later that online diarist Jorn Barger named it a *weblog*. In 1997, another user shortened it to *blog*, and in 2004, the *Merriam-Webster* dictionary declared *blog* the "word of the year."

In 1996, the Open Pages "webring" enabled web sites to be linked. Three years later, Pyra Labs gave people free server space and tools to create their own web sites. The blogging phenomenon now had wings. Boing Boing, one of the most-linked-to blogs in the world, was born with the new millennium. Two and a half years later, Blogads, the first broker of blog advertising, surfaced. Blogvertising took off during the 2004 Presidential election as it proved to be more effective than direct mail for politicians to reach young voters. In 2005, marketers spent $50 to $100 million to advertise on blogs.

Some companies, eager to join the party and make their brands part of the conversation, have sailed into the wild blog yonder by creating sections on their corporate web sites that invite and respond to public comments. In Nobullbar.com, Diageo executive vice president Guy Smith posts on policy issues about alcohol, like underage drinking. He identifies himself, links to external web sites, and answers even hostile questions lobbed his way. In 2005, General Motors vice chairman Bob Lutz began a weekly blog called FastLane that has made the stumbling giant appear, if not innovative, at least earnest and well-meaning.

The once ultrasecretive Boeing Company, which has found itself embroiled in well-publicized ethical and political scandals, got into smooth blog skyways after a rocky takeoff. When VP Randy Baseler began a blog around the company's view of aerospace, his brother bloggers roasted him for not allowing comments and for messengering rather than revealing. His early pitiful attempt was even derided as a embarrassment to the blogosphere. Baseler heeded the suggestions hurled his way and evolved the site to offer real insights and receive widespread praise. A second Boeing blog afforded the tens of thousands who logged on each month a rare look at how the manufacturer built and certified its 777 Worldliner, and a rare listen in such heretofore off-limits airspace as ethical compliance rules and management compensation.

IBM actually urges its workers to get out there and blog, and Microsoft employee Robert Scoble's self-deprecating postings have been credited with helping to reverse his employer's "evil empire" reputation. On the other hand, some companies have fired workers for musings they wrote on their personal blogs. They were irked at employees for revealing company secrets or stealing company time. The latter is endemic. *Ad Age* found that one in four American workers visits blogs while on the job and spends on average 3.5 hours, or 9 percent of the work week, scoping them. Blogads and Feedburner attest that traffic on blogs peaks during business hours.

Other companies have tried to squash blogs that have invaded what they consider their zone. As soon as FedEx caught whiff of a blog in which an Arizona man displayed oddball furniture he'd fashioned from FedEx boxes, the carrier invoked provisions of the Digital Millennium Copyright Act to force the site down. Bloggers saw it as an unnecessary show of force against a company fan.

Less drastic perhaps, but equally ostrich-like, initially Netflix spurned Mike Kaltschnee and the blog this ardent fan had created around Netflix. But as Hackingnetflix.com grew and attracted 250,000 visitors a month and appeared near the top on any online search for Netflix, the DVD rental store came to its senses.

Other companies, less inclined to expose themselves to stinging criticism in return for a dialogue that could prove wildly beneficial, have tried to conceal authorship. They've created fake blogs and character blogs and paid real-life bloggers to blog for them. Since 2004, BlogStar Network has paid bloggers to write positive comments about corporate sponsors without revealing these arrangements to readers. Darden restaurants used it to tout Bahama Breeze, spiking mentions of the 32-location chain. Recently, PersonalHomeMortgages.com was offering $8 to blogs that posted at least 100 words on how they simplify the mortgage process, and Pingo calling cards was paying $3 for a 100-word post with picture.

For the most part, bloggers resent marketers masquerading in sheep's clothing to hide their ulterior motives and bristle at their artificial language of exaggerated enthusiasm, which stands out against the personally written, conversational tones of most blogs. Bloggers disdain these stealth bloggers as manufactured, amateurish, clueless, and untrustworthy—and have given them a reception that's nasty, brutish, and short.

Dr. Pepper/7-Up's blog was one of the first to go sour. In 2003, to launch its new "milk-based drink with attitude," the company created a blog with Raging Cow's persona and courted young influential bloggers to hype the beverage. But Dr. P. didn't want these brand advocates to divulge who was prodding them, and the would-be nefarious arrangement blew up when blogs exposed it.

Reckitt Benckiser publicly apologized in 2005 when bloggers exposed that "Barry Scott," the fictional spokesman for its Cillit Bang European household cleaner had planted "comment spam" throughout cyberville. McDonald's was fried for pretending that a real human couple had found a McD fry that resembled Abe Lincoln and were blogging about it. In March 2006, *The New York Times* took Wal-Mart to task after bloggers used wording straight out of their press releases without citing the source. Bacardi also came under fire for fronting a 21-year-old "Bacardi blogging dude" it paid in bucks and booze to share his (edited) life online. Everything about its Betterthanbeer.com site reeked of legalese; it had obviously been filtered through Bacardi's PR team and most of it (including 14 of the first 19 posts) was instigated by the marketer.

Stealth blogging is dangerous business, especially when there's so little penalty for stepping out from behind the curtain. The Keller Fay Group found that the average American mentions specific brands 56 times a week, and that positive mentions outnumber negative six to one. People turned on by a company or product are far likelier to blog about it than those who are unhappy with it. That's more than cold comfort to corporations ceding some control by communicating on blogs.

Not long ago, Gawker Media vowed it would "never accept an ad from a domestic car manufacturer. We hate American cars and our readers do too," sales director Christopher Batty noted in his blog. The same went for big pharmaceutical companies, he said. "They don't want us, we don't want them: All our readers are healthy and beautiful." While Gawker may spurn ads, most blogs are dying for them. Happily for them, according to Forrester almost two out of three national marketers want to advertise here.

Some already do. Audi promoted its A3 model hatchback on 286 blogs—a three-month run that netted them 68 million pages for an outlay of just $50,000. That's a tenth of what it would have cost to run a banner ad for just a day on Yahoo!'s home page. Budget Car Rental ran a blog-only campaign involving a treasure hunt. Participants had to check its company-generated blog posts daily for clues leading them to various real-life locations.

In 2006, JWT bought all the ad space on liberal-leaning HuffingtonPost.com for a week to showcase its best commercials. It hoped to get bloggers to fall for the spots and send them to friends—and to demonstrate that the oldest ad agency in the United States was hip and rarin' to compete in nontraditional categories. Rocketboom.com auctioned off a week of advertising on its site (via eBay) for $40,000. Ninety percent of revenues for AndrewSullivan.com come from ads. And marketers spent more than $150,000 in 2005 to get before the (on average) 500,000 visitors per day to the Daily Kos.

Verifying blog audiences and determining that they're for real rather than, say, created by a spamming robot, is hardly failsafe. But more tools for marketers to map their way around this new terrain keep emerging. Google provides blog search and since June 2003 has matched ads to blog content. Technorati, Pubsub, and Icerocket monitor blog activity around keywords a company selects (including its own name). BuzzMetrics tracks word-of-mouth activity initiated by blogs. Talkdigger aggregates searches from several blog search engines and ranks the results by link popularity. Opinmind.com classifies blog search results by bias and Biz360 by activity that's "meaningful and actionable."

Feedster collects everything a blog has posted to profile it. If the blogger uses profanity or invented spelling or often wanders off topic, Feedster knows and lets advertisers determine what they can live with. (If something objectionable goes up on a blog, Feedster can pull their ad in seven minutes.) And a trade group to set measurement standards and perform research on blogs is in the works.

One area where marketers need no help is in recognizing that anyone, whether a peeved customer or ex-employee, can skewer their reputations and devastate their brands in the blogosphere. Sony BMG Music Entertainment found itself sideswiped after a blog reported that it was distributing spyware software on music CDs. Dell learned this the hard way after Jeff Jarvis, on his BuzzMachine blog, documented a string of mismanaged e-mails and phone calls as he tried to get Dell to fix his malfunctioning computer. The open letter he wrote Dell calling its PC "a lemon" and its customer service "appalling" became the third most linked-to post in the blogosphere the day after it was posted. Jarvis ultimately got a refund, but type the phrase "Dell hell" on Google now, and up pops 14.24 million results. Type "Dell sucks" and bingo, there's more than 3.8 million. (Any brand followed by the word *sucks* in Google seems to light a flame under a company.)

But blogs can actually help companies. In September 2004, word (and then a demonstrative video) raced through the blogosphere showing how Kryptonite's U-shaped locks could be easily picked with the plastic casing of a Bic pen. Kryptonite funneled the noise into an improved lock. Companies have used blog buzz to guide future product design, address what's on customers' minds, and fix a problem with a product. Surprisingly, blogs also seem to have cut calls to corporate help centers: Customers with problems often go to a blog they trust before phoning a company they're less sure about.

As more companies recognize that blogging as an institution is here to stay (while the old-time press embargo is on its way out), many are readying "lockbox blogs" as part of their crisis planning. Hidden behind an Internet firewall, these blog postings and videoclips prepared in advance can be made visible to the public at short notice. PR firms have departments to woo bloggers with access and information and product samples and gifts just as they talk to the mainstream media, which are themselves motoring down a narrowing road.

20

WHY *THE NEW YORKER* WAS TRASHED FOR TEAMING WITH TARGET

S ince its first issue on February 21, 1925, *The New Yorker* has established itself as a perennial leader of editorial integrity—the venerable, sophisticated, cosmopolitan, preeminent forum for serious journalism and fiction. "Not for the old lady in Dubuque," its debut issue famously declared. It became known for the monocled dandy espying a butterfly on its cover, its often-inscrutable cartoons, and for what writer James Wolcott describes as the "theatrical care" it devoted to the subtleties of communication, which included "the microscopic beauty of a properly placed comma." Public libraries used to keep bound volumes of this "cult object and coffee-table signifier of taste and breeding" behind the desk to prevent pages being razored out. It may be, Wolcott says, the sole magazine in the world to "inspire reverence and druidical devotion."

Yet the 80-something-year-old magazine, which had snagged 44 National Magazine Awards (more than any competitor by laps), seriously toyed with its reputation in mid-2005. In the August 22 issue, there were articles on Kinky Friedman and North Korea as a slave state as well as the usual *New Yorker* sections, departments, cartoons, and ads. But this time, every one of those ads was for Target. And every one was a whimsical illustration that more than coincidentally looked like it was editorial. All had Target's signature red-and-white circle, but none included the store's name. Even the cover, with red-and-white beach balls, suggested Target.

For almost as many years as *The New Yorker* has been publishing, the magazine industry has had guidelines separating editorial and advertising or what the industry calls church and state. Advertising must look sufficiently different from the editorial pages that readers can easily tell the difference. Advertorials must be slugged "advertisement" or "promotion." The front cover has been off limits.

It's one thing when a magazine like *Premiere* blurs that line. Its July/August 2006 issue featured an interview with a star of the film *Little Miss Sunshine* conducted by Howard Karren, a contributing editor to the magazine under a small "paid advertisement" disclaimer. It's quite a different matter when *The New Yorker* does it. With that stunt (which the publisher promised never to repeat), *The New Yorker* trifled with its hard-earned reputation as the bastion of editorial integrity, and with the very essence of what magazines are selling: truth and authority. While they lack the buzz of a cable food-fight show or reality TV blockbuster, they inspire confidence. Readers believe in them, trust them, and engage with them.

That responsibility, coupled with economic necessities, has wedged magazines between a boulder and a bigger boulder. Paper prices keep rising. So do postage and the cost of attracting new subscribers. Subscription cards that flutter out of magazines (and drive readers bonkers) generate on average 12 percent of new subscribers, down from about 20 percent a few years ago, at $5 to $10 each. The cost of signing subscribers through direct mail is often more than the subscription price. Direct mail now accounts for about 22 percent of new sales and is growing. The Internet generates around 10 percent of new subscribers. Newsstand sales return considerably more profit to the publisher.

That explains why in 2006 Meredith stopped selling *Child* and Hachette, *Elle's Girl* in their physical forms. It also explains why *Time* magazine shifted its on-sale date to Friday from Monday—to boost readership and attract advertisers who want to reach consumers before the weekend. (In 1997, *People* moved to Monday from Friday and news-stand sales soared.)

Odd as it may sound, other publishers have also slashed distribution of many titles to save money. *Time* cut its annual distribution to 22.5 million copies in 2005 from 32.5 million in 1997. *Self*, from Conde Nast, dropped to 11.4 million in 2005 from 13.5 million a decade before. And *ESPN, the Magazine* sent 2.5 million copies to newsstands last year from its peak of 8.4 million in 2000. *Playboy*, *Business Week*, and *Woman's Day* have all shrunk the circulation rate base they guarantee advertisers to weed out less-engaged readers. Five years ago, this would have caused a media buyer's eyebrow to rise; now media buyers look askance when the publishers announce circulation increases, wondering what tricks they've got up their sleeve to lure the additional readers.

While revenue for the industry has held steady because of price increases, advertising pages in the last few years have been flat or down. In fact, if it weren't for pharmaceutical advertising, the newsweeklies would be down to two, with *U.S. News & World Report* extinct. "New" media has pinched magazines' heels, with their ability to offer marketers instant feedback about the effectiveness of their ads—and instant opportunities to recast those ads if they're not working. Monthly magazines with lead-times of several weeks can't compete. (Help is on the way, however. In July 2006, a new Rapid Report allowed publishers to file circ figures on a per-issue basis and Readership.com, a new online audience measurement service, provides them with quick detailed readership data on each issue.)

At the same time, with the obvious exception of the shopping magazines like *Lucky*, product placement that is ubiquitous on TV has not yet impregnated magazines. *Yet* is the operative word. The trust that readers have in magazines is catnip to marketers, who relish their editorial endorsements. Indeed, when Toyota's Lexus proposed to several magazines that they put its cars in their editorial pages, the car company taunted them with details of how its vehicles were showcased on the reality-TV show *The Contender*. And it goaded them with talk of their own obsolescence. "I just don't think the traditional wall between magazine editorial and advertising units represents what's happening in the world today," sniffed Deborah Wahl Meyer, vice-president for marketing at Lexus.

That hurt an industry ultrasensitive about its "maturity." In exhorting his industry to get with the times, Magazine Publishers Association chairman Jack Kliger denounced the paid-circulation-rate-base-guarantee way it charges advertisers as "from an era that predates modern audience measurement metrics" and is irrelevant in calculating advertising ROI. Other media study impressions and ad effectiveness in a timely fashion. Magazines fight for ad dollars hobbled by metrics not comparable to them. Other media deal in audiences; magazines deal in paid circulation. (Audit Bureaus of Circulation (ABC), the industry police force, won't count those who read magazines in doctors' offices, for example.) In fact, the United States is the only country in the world with a rate-base system. (It was derived so advertisers did not have to wait for ABC audits a year later and because they wanted some assurance about upcoming circulation.)

Rate-base guarantees undersell engagement, which is the magazine industry's trump card and just what advertisers want at a time of unprecedented interruptive messages. A Northwestern University study defines magazines as the original on-demand medium, available on consumers' terms—whenever and wherever they choose—engaging while other media interrupt. Its study found that while consumers zap, mute, tune out, or fast-forward through TV commercials, block spam or pop-up ads online, and download music to avoid commercials, they regard ads in magazines as not merely acceptable, but an integral part of their reading experience. People talk enthusiastically about TV without commercials, but no one wants ad-free magazines, the study concluded.

Forward-thinking publishers have reached other conclusions about how to thrive in a new media age, one where, in 2006 for the first time, almost as many ad dollars went online as into magazines. They're experimenting with ways to be a brand, not a book. Dennis Publishing has ventured into producing products like hair dye and opened a chain of Maxim lounges across the country to host Maxim promotional events. *Sporting News*, born in 1886, developed a chain of SN-branded restaurants in Holiday Inns. *Playboy* systematically colonized clubs, web sites, cable TV, cell phone screens, and consumer goods. *Time* launched the edgy Office Pirates.com as an online-only magazine.

Sports Illustrated took a key asset, its swimsuit edition, and has posted it online with outtakes and additional content for subscribers before the print issue arrives in mailboxes. It also sells videos of the swimsuit photo shoot on iTunes. And in months concurrent with the spring and fall fashion and holiday seasons, ShopVogue.com showcases the booty of its magazine advertisers, with links for readers to buy.

Some magazines have gone even further, converting their web sites into online stores. Visitors to AmericanBabyShop.com can buy gifts featured in the magazine's pages. Hearst's now defunct *Shop Etc.* launched a virtual mall where advertisers rented "store space." The decorating magazine *Domino* maintains a wish list and gift registry around products advertised in its print magazine. And *Runners World* sold Asics and Adidas on sponsoring training podcasts for marathons, with motivational tips from past winners, advice on pre-race food, and course details.

Cosmo Girl sends daily horoscopes to cell phones for a small monthly fee. Would-be chefs who subscribe to *Gourmet* or *Bon Appetit* can browse a library of 20,000 meal ideas—and receive ingredient lists on their cell phones from Epicurious.com. Ratcheting up the interactivity beyond "letters to the editor," several titles invite readers to respond to polls via text message or e-mail. In addition to such startling photos as a rotting corpse and a woman immolating herself, *Shock*, the U.S. version of Hachette's French *Choc* magazine, offers web games and a way for readers to contribute their own shocking pictures at ShockU.com.

People engaged in real strategic ballet to protect the franchise it wrested from the tabloids. After it spent $4 million for the exclusive North American rights to the first photos of Shiloh Nouvel Jolie-Pitt, it devised an ambitious publicity plan to capitalize on its checkbook journalism. But days before *People's* official publication, the pictures of Angelina Jolie and Brad Pitt cuddling their new daughter appeared on Gawker, PerezHilton.com, and dozens of other blogs and web sites. (Some were taken from a bootleg copy of *Hello!* magazine, which had bought the photo rights in Britain; others were purloined.)

People's lawyers immediately fired off cease-and-desist letters, but they could just as easily have been thank-you notes. The editor appeared on *The Today Show*, the magazine jacked up its cover price, and rather than undermine *People*, the blogs actually drummed up even greater interest in its coverage, which led to larger newsstand sales.

Then there's *Forbes*, which in summer 2006 sold a significant minority stake in its then-storied 89-year-old magazine, much younger and flourishing web site, and a gaggle of smaller media properties to Elevation Partners, a private equity firm, with Bono, the singer from U2, as one of its partners.

Steve Forbes admitted that the company's old business model had been "blasted by the Web" as advertisers continued to flee print.

At the height of the technology boom, *Forbes* was the leading business news magazine. Getting ready to go public, it invested tens of millions of dollars in beefing up its digital diadem. The IPO never happened, but once the Web took off, so did the Forbes.com web site. It attracted traffic in all sorts of creative ways from editorial features on such wide-ranging topics as topless sunbathing and pay-for-click alliances with travel partners. The result is a web site with 10 million unique visitors a month, whereas the magazine had little more than half the advertising it had carried in its heyday. It's not hard to see that Elevation was buying into a web site with a magazine attached, rather than the other way around.

That online world is where magazines are increasingly going, although they'll remain a vibrant on-demand medium. New titles will constantly emerge, forcing the weaker ones in the field to reinvent themselves or die. Those barely hanging on will drop off. The survivors will be strong and healthy. Readers will continue to savor the personal time they spend with magazines and advertisers will continue to want to come along.

21

WHY OUR EYEBALLS
STOPPED COUNTING

S ince Court Television Network launched on July, 1, 1991, it has
become identified with trials of the rich and famous (Michael
Jackson) and the particularly vicious or snarky (Scott Peterson).
Although available in nearly 80 million homes, it has never been
a ratings blockbuster. At their peak, its highest-rated shows, the original
series *Forensic Files* and *Psychic Detectives* attracted at best 1.2 million viewers each.

In the spring of 2005, Court TV took a risky step concocting the mix
that it was offering viewers. It split into two distinct programming enti-
ties: daytime agenda, devoted to trial coverage and news, and its evening
and weekends block, given over to original narrative-drama reality and its
own tagline, "Court TV: Seriously Entertaining."

It took an even riskier step in what it was offering advertisers: both
the traditional guarantee of ratings points *and* a minimum of engaged
viewers—that is, that viewers will not only watch the programming but
that they'll watch the ads within it . . . guaranteed. Court TV had its back
to the wall. It needed to break from the welter of cable channels competing for ad dollars. If Court TV were to fall short on either front, it would
owe the advertiser a hefty "make-good" for free ad time. If it met its goal,
advertisers agreed to send more ads its way.

Happily for Court TV, 97 percent of its schedule met or exceeded what it had promised. Impressed, Pfizer upped its commitment to the network, and agreed to help sponsor the launch of the third season of its *Psychic Detectives*, including a *Psychic Circle* stunt at Time Warner, where 50 psychics read tarot cards, palms, and passersby's fortunes. IAG Research suggests that the show, about real-life crimes that psychics and law enforcement officers joined to solve, engages viewers more than the average broadcast show does: 10 percent higher when it comes to viewer attentiveness and 21 percent higher for brand recall of the commercials within the show.

Court TV has been peddling "involvement" for some time, claiming that viewers stay riveted to its investigative shows to learn "who done it" and that that intense focus transfers to the commercials surrounding the show. Only recently has the rest of the ad community caught up and come "courting." The rules of engagement have changed. In a headlong rush for accountability, *ROI* today could just as easily stand for return on involvement as return on investment.

Virtually since television flickered into America's living rooms more than half a century ago, advertising time on it has been sold on the basis of audience size translated into gross rating points and CPM (cost per thousand). But lately marketers have become less interested in the number of eyeballs that see a screen or hands that touch a page and more interested in the *behavior* of the owners of those hands and eyes, and how the ad message connects with them. The Advertising Research Foundation calls *engagement* "a search for twenty-first-century GRPs" (gross ratings points).

The conundrum that retail magnate John Wanamaker voiced almost a century ago—that half his marketing budget was wasted, he just didn't know which half—still weighs heavily on marketers today. But now, they've got the tools to find out.

The need has never been more pressing. A recent survey of CEOs identified their most urgent developmental priority as making their marketing more efficient. Under tremendous pressure to produce results pronto or vacate the chair, CEOs are demanding to know the return on every marketing dollar spent. Almost half of companies with sales above

$500 million are "creating a dashboard," lingo for a performance measuring system.

Advertisers have long distrusted the system. Costs for TV time kept climbing. The advertisers' voice has faded to dim: Wielding just the remote control, more than three out of four TV watchers often mute the sound during commercials or surf to other channels, or use that time to grab a snack or use the bathroom. Those with a digital video recorder largely skip the ads altogether. And even when they're watching, chances are it's not with their undivided attention: Studies show that the average American adult does 2.5 additional activities while taking in a TV show. (They're involved in *three* additional activities while surfing the Net.) Younger people cram in even more than the 39 hours of activity that the typical adult does in a day by constant multitasking.

At the same time, a plethora of other media highways, like video games and cell phones, have materialized and they provide real accountability. Clicks on the Internet indicate not just who is glancing at a web site, but who is engaged, who is acting on it. The closest TV has to demonstrate the effects of its "suggestions" are the Home Shopping Club and its clones, infomercials, and the late-night Ginsu-knife or BowFlex home gym–type direct-response ads or long-form infomercials.

Although disdained as media's cheapest slum, this "real estate" is gentrifying. The Little Giant Folding Ladder that rolls on built-in wheels and can hold a 300-pound man, and folds up and stores under the bed, still struts its stuff here, along with Proactiv Solution acne treatment (hawked by Jessica Simpson and Diddy), The Gazelle Freestyle exercise machine, and all manner of get-rich-quick schemes. But classy residents have started moving in. Procter & Gamble is promoting mainstream lines like Cover Girl, Iams, and Old Spice here. And the success of the George Foreman Grill made the neighborhood seem more eccentric than scruffy. Indeed, one in four American viewers has bought an infomercial product—which took advantage of their boredom—and the Leisure Trends group says viewers trust these long-form ads more than they trust Congress, used-car salesmen, or corporate executives.

Marketers trust them because feedback from them is instantaneous. Studies show that at least 85 percent of infomercial-inspired purchases are made within 10 minutes of the end of the program. That means, if it's not making the phone ring, it gets pulled . . . immediately.

In the Darwinian evolution of advertising, it's not hard to see why more and more commercials will incorporate some form of direct response like a toll-free number or URL.

Surprise, it seems, breaks though clutter because of something experts call *peripheral apperception*. When something on the fringes of your field of perception doesn't fit with what you expect, you are en garde. And when you see an ad for something you've been shopping for lately, but in a context where you don't expect to see it, it grabs your attention more than when you see the same ad in an environment where you expect to see it.

Another thing few can agree on is whether engagement with a medium has any spillover effect or whether media engagement and advertising engagement are different. If a person is absorbed by a show, article, song, or chat, does it follow that he or she will be immersed in the ads surrounding it?

A 2006 Starch Research study suggests not. Starch found that advertising in high-engagement magazines didn't perform any better than ads in magazines where the readers paid a lot less attention. Some miffed publishers snapped back that those findings defied common sense and were akin to claiming there's no definitive evidence that smoking causes cancer. Yet in homes with digital video recorders, shows that are said to be most engaging (high-rated sitcoms, dramas, and movies) are the most frequently time-shifted with the commercials fast-forwarded through.

The Weather Channel came out with a sunnier, self-fortifying conclusion. It found that deeper viewer involvement in a TV program, that is, watching with a purpose, translates into higher recall of ads in those shows and increased engagement with advertising. Not surprisingly, viewers tune to this channel for specific information that affects their lives; more than two times as many watch with a purpose as are deemed purposeful viewers of conventional TV.

Another reason why the eyeballs taking in shows (i.e., TV ratings) stopped counting as *the* way to price advertising is because researchers can now confirm who is actually staying put during a word from the sponsor. Nielsen now provides a "minute-by-minute" audience measurement to ascertain who is staying tuned. And PreTesting Co.'s Media-Check service has digital boxes in 35,000 households in a handful of cities wired to TVs to monitor how the people who own those sets respond to ads, both on live TV and in programs taped on digital video recorders. Daily tallies let advertisers decide to put more money behind winners, or kill losers or try them in different time slots.

Burger King discovered that while admeisters applauded its ad where members of the fictional Coq Rock rock band donned chicken masks, viewers did not. Less than half the number of those who stayed through a conventional Burger King spot followed this one (6 vs. 12 percent).

A 2005 MediaCheck test in Omaha revealed that the main reason viewers skipped ads was that the spots were dull or tired—that they'd seen them too often. (MediaCheck can also induce ad viewing by "paying" consumers with coupons, product samples, or discounts. In the Omaha test, 52 percent of the coupons printed were redeemed—50 times the national rate for newspaper coupons.)

MediaCheck is on to something, recognizing that there are lots of ways to change a channel, or in this case, engage a viewer. And their way may well become the highway. After all, we all know that no commercial is effective if people don't see it. A market as fluid as the one we're living in needs predictive tools to ensure that when the marketer builds it, they will come.

22

WHY THE SMART MONEY MOVED ITS CHIPS FROM POKER TO BULLS

Think of the $250 billion sports marketing universe as a solar system. The national football league is the sun around which the (now eight) planets revolve. Baseball, basketball, college varsity, and NASCAR are the gas giants in its orbit. Then come the still-bright but lesser planetoids: hockey, golf, tennis (particularly around the time the U.S. Open and Wimbledon hit), and soccer (the largest worldwide sport but somewhat disdained in the United States). And, of course, the Olympics (primarily) and the World Cup (secondarily) shine brightly every two years and four years respectively. Then there are the ever-present plutessimals, like the America's Cup, which Ted Turner's achievement glamorized, although sailing never attracted major audience interest.

Let's focus for a moment on the comets, which flash brilliantly before fading. That is what poker is, and was, and what professional bull riding (PBR) seems destined to be. So bright is PBR's arc, you can consider it the 2008 Haley's.

Big-money poker shone like an asteroid in the early 2000s. It was everywhere on TV and the Internet. PartyPoker.com was hosting about

32 hands of poker play per second, amounting to about $45 billion wagered for the year, and there were thousands of other online poker sites. As late as May 2006, Fox unveiled the new high-stakes "Poker Dome Challenge."

The 1965 movie, *The Cincinnati Kid*, with Steve McQueen as the unflappable prince of poker, may have planted the seed of this phenomenon. In 2002, the introduction of a hole-card camera that let TV viewers peek at heretofore hidden cards in players' hands gave it the equivalent of a steroid boost. Pokermania solidified with the 2003 debut of *Showdown*, as normal, everyday folks could visualize themselves as the sport's Michael Jordans. After all, 27-year-old nebbish accountant Chris Moneymaker had parleyed $40 in his PokerStars.com account into a $2.5 million win at the World Series of Poker in Las Vegas.

In 2005, poker players worldwide spent $376.6 million collectively buying their way into live games, more than five times what they'd "invested" in 2001. PokerPages.com, which tracks the industry, reported that about twice the number of people entered tournaments in 2005 as in 2001 (304,500 vs. 147,500) and that the number of those queuing up for the World Poker Tour had swelled more than sevenfold to 10,000 in 2006 from 2003. To today's college kids, online poker (particularly Texas Hold 'em) is as much a part of campus life as bingeing on beer and cutting lecture classes. These "academics" are part of the masses who in 2005 bet $60 billion in online poker games.

But, can you see them, the cracks in the façade that are beginning to surface? Like the last Roman tired of watching gladiators fed to the lions, there's a simmering but growing detachment among fans, suggesting that poker is more a fad than entertainment with legs. The Travel Channel's ratings for its *World Poker Tour* fell 36 percent in the last two years. Audiences for ESPN's *World Series* and for *Celebrity Poker Showdown* have similarly atrophied. The U.S. government's stance on the illegality of online poker has help clamp the growth. Recognizing the clear script on the wall, entrepreneurs who initially pitched poker to the TV networks are now hustling to develop darts, dominoes, and blackjack tournaments as the next sports luminary to replace the one that's ebbing.

They may be too late; something else has slipped into this astral plane. Willie Nelson and Waylon Jennings warned mammas not to let their babies grow up to be cowboys. America's new fascination with the Professional Bull Riders Tour suggests that neither those mammas nor their babies were listening. Perhaps nursed on John Travolta's suave performance in *Urban Cowboy*, they've become furtive wannabees. Millions of fans, east of the Mississippi as well as in the Wild West, are galvanized watching guys try to hang on for eight seconds atop the meanest, whirlingest, most cantankerous and ferocious creature on earth.

The rider may not drop his rope or with his free hand touch the "animal athlete," as these ranked and celebrated tons of muscular testosterone are called by the "buckle bunny" cult who follow their tour. (These criers with their pairs of lethal bayonets are responsible for half a rider's score vis-à-vis a degree-of-difficulty component such as that used in Olympic sports.) The eight seconds (or less) performance melds seamlessly with our attention deficit society.

When the Colorado-based Professional Bull Riders Association, formed in 1992 and still owned and operated by its athletes, crowned its first World Champion in 1994, the PBR's major tour consisted of eight events that offered a combined $250,000. Today, it's a 29-city, $10 million tour watched by some 100 million viewers on NBC Sports and the Outdoor Life Network. More than 1.1 million people attended its U.S. events in 2006, and by 2007, twice that number were expected to gawk in person at what has always been the most popular event in traditional rodeo.

This ultimate display of machismo is riding so high it may even get on the same track as NASCAR, whose fan base it shares and on whose growth strategy it has modeled its own. Like stock-car racing, it has migrated from the South outward by entertaining families. And like NASCAR, it has maximized sponsor participation: Racecars and their drivers have been likened to rolling billboards and virtually every media exposure references the sponsors. But with all its stomping and goring and treating participants as if they were rag dolls, PBR is a lot more dangerous than NASCAR, whose drivers after all use two hands and wear fireproof jumpsuits, helmets, and even cups (vs. just chaps, a protective vest, and a cowboy hat). And, of course, NASCAR has no clowns entertaining the crowd with some comic relief punctuating the tension. Amazingly, PBR is endorsed by several Christian ministries that view the bull riders' meekness, not weakness, as spiritual, and that hold church services in conjunction with PBR events.

The popularity of bull riding has its roots in the many livestock and rodeo shows around the country, where in many markets (witness the Houston Livestock and Rodeo Show) these are the top spectator events on the annual landscape. Since 2003, Ford has been chief sponsor of "the toughest sport on dirt's top circuit." Its pickups are showcased at the Built Ford Tough Series. Half of PBR fans own pickups, and about 40 percent of those are Fords. The top winner in Ford's battleforthebull.com contest wins part ownership in a prize bull. Other rough-and-rugged sponsors include Jack Daniels, Oberto Beef Jerky, the U.S. Army, Enterprise Rent-a-Car, Daisy air guns, Wrangler, Anheuser-Busch, Yamaha, Stetson, Salem cigarettes, Frito-Lay, Las Vegas, and the Mandalay Bay Resort in Las Vegas

Today, the sports marketing industry is a veritable media channel by itself. Some trace its origins back to the 1880s, when tobacco companies inserted cards of baseball players into cigarettes packs, a practice that evolved first into bubble-gum cards and ultimately into sports cards. The industry received a steroid shot in 1936, when Jesse Owens received free Adidas shoes to compete in the Berlin Olympics. By the time Muhammad Ali was a fixture in the ring, viewers had become schooled in noticing that his shoes were Adidas and his boxers, Everlast.

With tobacco companies' quasi-volunteer banishment from TV in 1971, they funneled millions of freed-up ad dollars into getting backdoor access. By sponsoring the Virginia Slims Tennis Circuit, for example, Philip Morris played by the rules and still got serious face time on TV sporting events. At the same time, athletes like O.J., "Broadway Joe" Namath, and Mean Joe Green emerged as product endorsers. The sneaker wars kicked off and tapped the marquee value of star jocks. The first all-sports network, ESPN, was born, and Rich Foods Inc. paid $1.5 million to name the first corporate-sponsored stadium in Buffalo, New York. By the 1980s, superstars of sports and sports marketing, like Michael Jordan and

Magic Johnson, had become superstars of pop culture as well. Anheuser-Busch spends about $300 million on sports-related advertising each year.

In the United States, of course, the apex of sports marketing is the Super Bowl, followed by the Olympics and World Series games. (The second tier includes the Daytona 500, Final Four, and NBA Finals.) But worldwide it's the World Cup. (Led by Hispanic devotees, the once long-resistant United States is just beginning to catch soccer fever.) The summer 2006 Cup attracted an audience of more than five billion viewers over four weeks. Some 300 million tuned in for the final game alone.

The Cup also attracts a galaxy of marketers eager for a sales kick from being associated with the event. Because it is so sponsor friendly, with far fewer restrictions on where and how companies can advertise than the Olympics, say, 21 official partners and suppliers paid soccer's world governing body, the Federation Internationale de Football Association, more than $1 billion for a tie-in. FIFA also took in more than $1.2 billion for worldwide television rights.

Anheuser-Busch, one of the seven U.S. companies among the 15 official sponsors, viewed the Cup as a way to reach beer drinkers in the 70 other countries where it sells Budweiser. Others, like McDonald's, which sponsored children escorting players onto the field, and Coca-Cola, which toured the Cup trophy worldwide and paid bloggers to chronicle the games and goings-on, used it as a jumping-off point to further engage their fans. Adidas made the Cup its platform to launch a $200 million ad campaign. Gillette, Avaya, MasterCard, Yahoo!, Emirates Airlines, Hyundai, and Fuji were among others forking over $45 million to $50 million for exclusive rights to the World Cup name and billboards in stadiums. Nike, by plastering its iconic Swoosh on the jerseys of eight qualifying teams, also scored its goals. The next World Cup, in South Africa, will be costlier for advertisers and even more awaited by fans. Long-time sponsor MasterCard was already bumped by rival Visa, which signed a deal with FIFA for 2010 and 2014 for close to $100 million.

Technology has changed the face of both sports and sports marketing. Fans can follow their teams' games and instantly find out anything about the players. Marketers have adapted, changing the jocks (now it's Tiger Woods, LeBron James, and Maria Sharapova who are the big draw) and more importantly how they connect with fans. For example, Sprint offers its 24 million customers a free NFL fantasy tracker. When a top player scores, they receive a celebratory text message, or they can elect to receive a red-zone alert when their favorite team gets inside the 20-yard line. They can also receive the game live on the third screen, manage fantasy teams, and cast their ballot in the Pro Bowl. T-Mobile customers can download NBA content and vote for the All-Star game, and on the basketball league's web site find blogs, podcasts, and video-clips of the plays of the day.

PART THREE

TOMORROW

23

What's Really Sexy about Porn? (A Peek at What's to Come)

If you want to know what media will look like tomorrow, look at what the sex industry is up to today. Even before the get-rich-quick schemers jump in, porn has landed, almost always the first application a new medium gets.

It's also often the most used. For a new technology to get adopted it needs fans and a compulsion to do it. Sex provides that. What else, people ask, could keep someone with a slow connection in the days of dialup waiting for a choppy postage-stamp-sized movie to load? And because it's often excluded from the mainstream channels, pornographers are always on the lookout for new, exciting ways around their restrictions.

From early days of civilization the "adult industry" has driven technological advances. John Tierney, in his 1994 article, "Porn, the Low-Slung Engine of Progress," described how centuries before ceramics technology was used to make utilitarian pots, artists clay-fired "Venus" figurines of women with exaggerated breasts and bottoms. Archeologists have deduced that sexual acts were among the first subjects artists depicted on cave walls, and the oldest known literature, recorded by the Sumerians in cuneiform on clay tablets, includes poetry celebrating a vulva. Not long after Gutenberg's press brought the written word to the masses in the late 1400s, lovemaking positions were selling more briskly than Bibles. Porn helped develop such techniques of fiction as dialogue and scene-setting. *Pamela*, recognized as the first English novel, came out in 1740; eight years later so did the first pornographic one, *Fanny Hill*.

Barred by the government from radio and television, pornographers developed new audio and visual technologies. In 1978, when not even 1 percent of American homes had videocassette recorders and Hollywood spurned the new technology, more than three out of four videocassettes sold were pornographic. Indeed, the first one on the market in 1977 featured couples going at it.

When cable systems opened their airways to public-access programming, pornographers surged forward with skin shows. In 1894, the first general-interest movie was shown in America. In 1896, a porn flick was open to the public for the first time. To date, supposedly, more pornographic movies than nonpornographic ones have been filmed. The camcorder and instamatic camera were quickly seized by amateur home-porn enthusiasts to make hay at home. (Do you think it was coincidence that the first affordable Polaroid model was named "The Swinger"?)

Since the dismantling of the Bell phone system in 1984, purveyors of phone sex rolled out pay-per-call services and videophone sex. Phone sex has been richly profitable since the 1980s, prodding providers to upgrade their infrastructure.

Smut also perked up the World Wide Web (and sales of the routers, servers, and software that thrive on it) by inventing security in transactions and building consumer confidence about online use of credit cards and other e-commerce payment systems. Online pornographers' early experiments with fee-based subscriptions, pop-up ads, and electronic billing have been adopted by Fortune 500 companies. Porn sites, with their need to deliver big sex pictures fast, were early users of audio and video streaming and web pay-per-view and they forced upgrades in servers, data systems, and broadband so users could better enjoy their images of copulation.

Many believe that chat and forums about sex were the umbilical cords that sustained America Online in its early days. Certainly, they were the molders of menus and interactivity. An early CD-ROM featured models changing poses instantly in response to commands from the viewer, acting as a *Penthouse* photographer. And they've made real headway in "blind linking," cooperating with rival sites to share traffic and get paid for the referral in an affiliate network and through reciprocal links. (And, of course, advertising from the more than $13-billion-per-year porn business, whose revenues top those of the NBA and all of pro football, has fattened the profits of companies like Yahoo!)

Recently adult-content sites have advanced the development of new informal partnering, outsourcing, upselling, and site tracking. They've embraced podcasting and webcams, adapted imaging to tiny screens for mobile-phone downloads, and are the prime driver of third-generation (3G) mobile services demand. And their use of titillation by the meter—peek fast—suggests that media, like Genoa salami at the deli counter, will be priced by quantity. At Sweet Sixteen parties of the future, the coveted gift will be 1,000 media minutes. And your media bill of tomorrow will probably look a lot like your phone bill today (and probably be as incomprehensible).

Carat (Can Anyone Really Anticipate Tomorrow?) knows that no one can predict the future of media, but history suggests that sex will continue to lead it with digiflesh web sites functioning as glorified test labs for emerging technology.

Something else will lead it: marketers with moxie. Every day for the past half-century, millions of Americans watched transfixed the goings-on in TV's fictional Midwestern town of Oakdale. Procter & Gamble birthed *As the World Turns* in 1956, and has been producing soap operas since it invented the genre for radio in 1933, with *Oxydol's Own Ma Perkins*. But just as the world's largest advertiser was avant-garde then, so it is now, podcasting audio versions of the soaps, staging Internet-based lottery-style promotions, soliciting user-generated content with a "Create Our Ad" contest for Dawn grease fighter, running ads for Crest on cell phones, leading in word-of-mouth marketing with the creation of "Tremor" for teens in 2001, and "Vocalpoint" for moms in 2005, and shifting vast amounts from traditional into new media to reach consumers when and where they are most receptive. In 2005, P&G moved 8 percent of its U.S. marketing budget away from television and was doing likewise in Europe.

P&G and other forward-thinking companies recognize that we're smack dab in the midst of a media revolution, and, while Carat can't predict all the winners (some hadn't even been conceived when we wrote this book), we know that online and search will be in that golden circle and that broadcast television will not. TV will remain king, but its empire will have been decolonized, a platform that allows shows to be created for distribution on DVD, VOD cable, and satellite services and portable devices like cell phones.

Most of it will be on-demand, meaning that you'll push a button to order a movie or download a video. Networks will shudder, because when prime time becomes "your time," their schedules become irrelevant. But advertisers will smile, for this is more fertile soil in which to plant messages as it reaches those already interested in a subject—like cooking—and because they can embed their food-tip and recipe messages in the programming. (VOD also affords much more precise feedback of who is watching what.)

McKinsey & Co. thinks that by 2010 (after factoring in increases in cost, saturation, and switching off of ads, and decreases in attention paid to them because of more multitasking) traditional TV advertising will be one-third as effective as it was in 1990. From 1995 to 2005, real ad spending on prime time rose 40 percent while audiences dropped by almost half. Look at teens, and conventional TV's future appears even darker. They spend less than half as much time watching TV as typical adults do and 600 percent more time online.

It was Thomas Friedman who charted our civilization's path from the

Iron Age to the Industrial Age to the Information Age to the Age of Interruption. That was yesterday, Tom.

We're moving into the age of relevance. People don't hate ads; they hate irrelevant disruption. Advertisers get permission by being relevant. TV advertising will be an all-new sales channel. Instead of buying a flight of television commercials, Carat and other media buyers will purchase access to people's intentions created through search history and TV viewing habits. Advertisers will advertise only to the interested and in the process eliminate massive waste. The ad industry will get bigger as more advertisers will see its efficiencies for a lot less money. Search will evolve to service on a silver platter. Rather than have answers spat back in response to a typed-in term, they'll be presented in a customized way based on the typist's usage or behavior. It will be personalization, more than search. And it will be the center of the universe of *intent-based* marketing.

Commerce and cause will merge, where institutions like St. Jude Children's Research Hospital forsake the tin cup in lieu of corporate partners as it is doing with its innovative "Thanks for Giving" promotion. Experiential marketing, where customers come into more physical contact with brands, and gaming with products integrated into the play will accelerate. And wireless will be everywhere at the point of sale so you can get information, shopping lists, and coupons at the grocer.

Where a communication will appear will dictate its creative, versus the other way around. Media people don't fear testing, measurement, and numbers, the way creative folks do. Every plan will have metrics attached to it. Technology will have tumbled the old mediatocracy; the citizenry armed with their gadgets will represent the new. They'll control what they see and when, and that means advertising, too.

The media plan of the future will have fewer dollars going into TV and many more going into online with a company's web site more central than ever. The media plan of the future will reflect the ethnic makeup and cultural mosaic in America, where 47 million Americans or 17 percent of the population does not speak English at home. The media plan of the future will have more interactive elements: TV, radio, digital, online, experimental and sports marketing, direct marketing, direct mail, and PR and special events. The media plan of the future will look like the tiles of your bathroom floor, a series of components fit together seamlessly to create a cohesive marketing whole.

Marketers won't necessarily be left in the dust, though they'll have to quicken their pace to hold stride. Technology will help them too: They'll know what commercials work best against what audience and how best to target particular viewers. They'll be able to determine the ROI of every marketing dollar spent. And they'll try all manner of marketing from product placement to magazine advertorials to scale the new barricades. For example, on September 10, 2006, every half-hour, all 1,100 Clear Channel radio stations ran two-second "blink" ads for that night's premiere of the Fox comedy *The Simpsons*. Like pop-ups on the Internet, they're tough to avoid because by the time you try, they're over. A Ford spot on *American Idol* was shot to look like part of the show to keep viewers from zapping. Advertisers have begun negotiating for first or last placement in each commercial pod, to be seen before the remote is grabbed or as the show resumes.

Nielsen's fledgling measurement of audiences of commercials will go from a blunt tool (it started out providing only average ratings for commercials in an entire program) to a precise instrument, rating individual spots as is done in Europe and Asia. We'll see many more exciting movie commercials on TV: Viewers like them and they make commercial inventory overall more valuable. We'll see more live events and serialized plots to keep viewers faithful (vs. self-contained plots in each episode as in *C.S.I.*), as ads are best viewed during them. We'll see more corporate TV docudramas like *Unwrapping Macy's*, that combine the realism of a documentary with infomercial salesmanship. And in this era of brand democratization and citizen marketing, we'll see a whole lot more viewer e-mail and other participation on news shows.

We'll also see hyperlocalism and personalization, as if Connie Chung were ringing your doorbell. What happened in the Pikes Peak region of Colorado in spring 2006 will happen everywhere. A local online-only newspaper, "The High Plains Messenger," based in Colorado Springs, emerged, a community-driven virtual newspaper with local issues, investigative journalism, citizen journalism, arts and nightlife coverage, breaking news from the Associated Press, and podcasts.

We'll see elected mediatocracies spread their wings. The highly popular MySpace.com declared intentions to extend to a record label, film production company, and satellite-radio station and maybe a mobile service and ink-on-paper magazine. And we'll see marketers attempt to fashion their own media hits. The day after Super Bowl XLI, February 5, 2007, Anheuser-Busch introduced Bud TV.

There'll be lots more options, not just because with the less constrained distribution of the Web more voices than corporate media giants will be heard, but because with digital TV there will be four times the number of TV signals as there were in 2006, offering 24/7 news, all-weather, all-traffic, and all-music-all-the-time channels for their spectrum. High-def radio will also double the number of radio stations and many more cable channels will mean more programming and inventory. And with low-cost entry there'll be online magazines with every conceivable angle. ("Four Weeks" magazine, launched September 2006, is synchronized to a woman's monthly menstrual cycle with different articles depending on what hormones are streaming through the female body at that time of the month.)

Even as limitless possibilities replace bounded choices, there'll still be water-cooler conversation based on shared experience (from terrorism to Tom Cruise). At the same time, the megahit mentality encapsulated by who shot J.R. will be overshadowed by more people spending more time in virtual gathering places with those who share their special interests. And web-stores will satisfy the millions who can't find what they're looking for in brick-and-mortar stores. (At least one out of three books Amazon sells you won't find on the shelves of even the biggest real-world superstore.)

Audience numbers for all this content will be smaller but more valuable because there'll be no wastage. To target the toothless, PolyGrip won't buy Katie Couric: At least 90 percent of the *CBS Evening News* audience has teeth.

The metric of the future will be percent of the audience that's relevant (those with the going, growing prostate problem for Avodart), and involved. TV will usher those interested in the message to a new location for a one-on-one conversation. The 30-second ad that was once the beginning, middle, and end of the contact with the viewer will be a door opener, the beginning of a longer and possibly ongoing relationship with the prospective customer. With the blurring of media, old definitions of *magazine* or *newspaper* or *television* or *direct mail* will become meaningless. (Is a digital magazine or web site or e-mailed copy still a magazine?)

What we predicted more than a dozen years ago—that the passive era of TV would cede to a more participatory medium where shows must wait to be invited into people's living rooms—has happened. So has this scenario: It's 9:00 P.M., in Mill Valley, California. Veronica Miller is taking her husband Rob to task for his work-related absences and failure to pitch in around the house. Now that she's eight months pregnant she sure could use the help. Why Rob hasn't even read the copy of *What to Expect When You Are Expecting* that she'd put in his briefcase four months ago.

Rob cringes and slinks over to the computer. After checking his e-mail, guilt prompts him to search the Web—the sum total of human knowledge sitting in a box outside his kitchen—to smarten up. He orders a replacement copy of the book from Amazon and Googles "pregnancy baby." On the first link, Babycenter.com, he breezes through what to expect in this home stretch before pursuing a link advising him of 10 things he can do to be a better husband. Then he proposes seeing if something prenatal is on TV.

In marketing, this is a moment of aperture, just like the guys selling umbrellas outside train exits in the rain. It's the right product, at the right time, marketed to a prospect with the right mindset.

Rob clicks on his TiVo home page and types in "parent, childbirth, newborn" into the search-based interface to find five shows next week that fit the bill. He instructs TiVo to download them all and notes that one will be available in 30 minutes. Cookies in both his computer and TV have taken note of his programming selections and taken several marketing-orientated actions by cross referencing these picks with Rob's recent TV search history. The cookies share information with a marketing application run on Rob's computer, called GDS (Google Desktop Search). Altered by the marketing potential from the actions taken by Rob, GDS instantly uploads the new tags into Google's central advertising marketplace, where millions of *potentials* are aggregated and presented to thousands of advertisers for sale in a modified real-time auction. Most of the participating advertisers have preset their spending levels, their demographic preferences, and most importantly, their intent-based profiles.

While the Millers watch the show that Rob asked TiVo to download, a small box appears in the bottom of the screen announcing that several advertisers have appeared in their feed. Rob and Veronica pause the show, hit a button, and scan the doorbell-ringers. This is advertising to the interested. They pass on Gerber's offer of a free month of formula as they've decided to breastfeed, but opt in for a free box of Pampers, clicking a button to give delivery details to a Pampers fulfillment center. Then comes the killer ad: Click here for $50 off a Peg Perego stroller, the $350 Mercedes Benz of strollers. Both Rob and Veronica have heard of the Peg Perego—it is the talk of their friends from the Lamaze class. Veronica snuggles closer and wonders if they should go for it. Faced with this collision of brand advertising, direct marketing, data analytics, and technology deployed with a purpose, you know what they decide.

Now it's time for the industry to decide how to best advance that scenario. We think it's by joining in an open participation approach, banding together, reinventing, discussing, debating, and shaping the future of the advertising industry that's not dying but morphing. We see reforestation, not the creeping in of a desert landscape into advertising. That's why Carat created the Carat Exchange, so competitor experts in advertising can work together on the next generation of new media technologies and avoid what happened with the Internet.

In the early days of the World Wide Web, advertisers and their agencies stood on the sidelines. The technology developers and the advertising industry rarely met or spoke. Banner ads were conceived with little under-standing of CPMs and pricing and little sense of how they'd address the needs of advertisers. What marketer would ever voluntarily endorse the thumb-sized Internet banner ad? The early stage Internet bubble burst in large measure because there was no clear plan how web sites would be-come profitable without a more effective advertising model. Now we're working with YouTube on where to put advertising: *Before* holds up the user's experience; *during the middle* interrupts it; and posting it *at the end* is fu-tile—the user is gone. Carat has created videos for Adidas that are part of the content that users come there for.

Wall Street has special periods called *triple witching hours* where three factors merge to create a volatile market. The media world stands at one of those moments now with consolidation, globalization, and technology the prods. There has been more change in the past 24 months than in the past 24 years in this world. Change in the next 24 months will be just as significant, scary, unstable, eventful, fruitful, ex-citing, imaginative, and innovative, and the effects on our world, sim-ply profound. In the face of this whirlwind, with so many ways to reach prospective customers constantly emerging, few can go it alone. Even with a guide at their side steering them through a very tricky, rapidly evolving communications environment, marketers will struggle with analysis paralysis, and at the very least get used to being perma-nently uncomfortable.

We don't know what it is yet, but we do know that there's *something be-yond digital* that will make digital look like analog. We do know that we need to adapt to whatever it is and that what we do today may not work in a year or two. But we're assembling the toolkit, codifying Carat so that it stands for: Collaboration, Accountability, Rationality, Accessibility/ap-propriateness, and Timeliness/technique.

In his 1957 best-seller, *The Hidden Persuaders*, Vance Packard explored how mediameisters manipulated people to induce desire for products. He saw consumers as cooperative puppets, guided not by logic but by profes-sional persuaders who knew exactly what made them tick and how to make them jerk.

Semiotic theory echoes this refrain, considering consumers "cultural effects" more than "prime causes." According to Virginia Valentine, president of Semiotic Solutions, "consumers are not independent spirits, articulating their own original opinions and making their own individual buying decisions but are constructed by the communications of [popular] culture." Marketers who believe that, and media that continue to treat them as eaters, watchers, players, and viewers instead of producers, distributors, and even marketers, are toast.

INDEX